Table of Contents

Appendices

Chapter 1:

Introduction, Purpose of Nutrient Analysis, and Learning Outcomes

---

CHAPTER OBJECTIVES

After reading this chapter, you will understand how to:

- Relate the USDA school meal patterns to national nutrition standards for healthy children, such as the Dietary Guidelines for Americans and the Dietary Reference Intakes.
- Select an option for assessing compliance with Dietary Specifications requirements during an Administrative Review.

Introduction

The Final Rule for USDA's *Nutrition Standards in the National School Lunch and School Breakfast Programs, (published January 26, 2012) intends to ensure the provision of nutrient-dense meals (high in nutrients and low in calories) that meet the health needs of school children and reflect the most current dietary science.* Under the rule, all schools must follow a Food-Based Menu Planning (FBMP) approach for the National School Lunch Program (NSLP) and for the School Breakfast Program (SBP) and produce enough food to offer each child the quantities specified in the meal pattern. State agencies (SAs) may be required to conduct weighted nutrient analyses of school lunches and breakfasts for students in grades K through 12 as part of the Administrative Review (AR). Although School Food Authorities (SFAs) are not required to conduct nutrient analyses, they are expected to follow the meal pattern in order to meet nutrient

Nutrition Goals

Protein, Vitamins & Minerals

- Appropriate for age/grade group
- Minimize inadequacy

Calories

- Appropriate for age/grade group
- Reduce childhood hunger and prevent childhood obesity

Dietary Guidelines for Americans

- Eat a variety of foods, especially dark green, red, and orange vegetables; beans and peas; whole grains; and fat-free or low-fat milk and milk products
- Balance calories and physical activity to manage weight
- Consume at least half of all grains as whole grains
- Reduce sodium to < 2300 mg per day
- Limit saturated fat to < 10% of calories
- Keep *trans* fat consumption as low as possible
- Reduce the intake of solid fats and added sugars
- Choose foods that provide more potassium, dietary fiber, calcium, and vitamin D

Pre-Publication Copy

targets. However, SFAs may conduct nutrient analyses of meals to determine if they are in compliance with the required Dietary Specifications.

Nutrition Standards for Healthy Children

Nutrition Goals

The Nutrition Standards for school meals underscore our national responsibility to provide healthy school meals that are consistent with the Dietary Reference Intakes (DRIs), energy requirements for each age/grade group, and the Dietary Guidelines for Americans. The Standards are a critical component of combating the childhood obesity epidemic, while also addressing childhood hunger.

Menu Planning and Nutrient Analysis

See Appendix A for meal pattern requirements.

The meal pattern requires specific foods (components) and food quantities based on the age/grade of students. The State agency will conduct menu reviews, which may include performing a weighted nutrient analysis of the lunch and breakfast menus offered for each age/grade group during the review period to determine compliance with the Dietary Specifications for calories, saturated fat, and sodium. State agencies will target a menu review site based on the Meal Compliance Risk Assessment Tool and select one of four options to complete the Dietary Specifications and Nutrient Analysis portion of the AR.

State agencies must select one of the following four options to assess compliance with dietary specifications:

- *Option 1: Complete the Dietary Specifications Assessment Tool*

  Complete the Dietary Specifications Assessment Tool (available at: http://www.fns.usda.gov/school-meals/administrative-review-manual) to determine the level of risk for meeting the dietary specifications based on the assessment of specific food service practices for lunch and breakfast. This option requires off-site review procedures prior to the on-site visit including the review of menu documentation.

- *Option 2: Validate an SFA-Conducted Nutrient Analysis*

  Validate an existing nutrient analysis that was conducted by the SFA or a contractor hired by the SFA. **A breakfast and lunch nutrient analysis performed using USDA-approved software must be available specifically for the**

targeted menu review site for the State agency to select this option. The State agency may accept the nutrient analysis after validating that the analysis was conducted in accordance with these Nutrient Analysis Protocols. An aggregated, district-wide analysis is not acceptable for validation.

- *Option 3: Conduct a Nutrient Analysis*

  The State Agency may decline to use the off-site Dietary Specifications Assessment Tool to determine the level of risk prior to the on-site visit. The State agency will then conduct a lunch and breakfast nutrient analysis using USDA approved software for the site selected for the targeted menu review.

- *Option 4: Alternate Method Using Menu Planning Tools Approved for Certification for Six Cents Reimbursement*

  State agencies may request approval from FNS to use an alternate methodology to assess compliance with dietary specifications requirements (see memo SP 46-2013 for more details).

NOTE: This manual will be used for all options when a nutrient analysis is conducted or validated to ensure the correct nutrient analysis protocols are followed.

When it is determined nutrient analyses are required, the State agency must refer to and follow the Nutrient Analysis and Validation Checklist (Appendix B). The checklist provides a series of questions to ensure specific requirements are met before a nutrient analysis is performed or validated. The checklist will prompt the State agency to complete the on-site portion of the Dietary Specifications Assessment Tool as it will provide useful information when conducting or validating the nutrient analyses.

Purpose of Nutrient Analysis

The purpose of nutrient analysis is to **determine compliance with regulatory requirements for calories, saturated fat, and sodium, and to monitor levels of these dietary components in school meals.**

Performing an accurate nutrient analysis is critical to the evaluation of menus and menu documentation. This manual is designed to provide the knowledge and skills to perform an accurate nutrient analysis.

Pre-Publication Copy

Learning Outcomes

The information contained in this manual will enable readers to:

1. Explain the purpose of a nutrient analysis and the nutrition goals of the USDA Nutrition Standards.
2. Select USDA-approved nutrient analysis software which will meet the needs of the State agency.
3. Describe key nutrient analysis points for schools to consider when selecting food items and quantities from the Child Nutrition (CN) Database.
4. Assemble materials necessary to conduct or validate a nutrient analysis.
5. Correctly enter data for food items (ingredients), recipes, menus, and school/SFA data following nutrient analysis protocols for school nutrition programs.
6. Discuss common data entry errors and how to prevent/identify mistakes.
7. Perform nutrient analyses, evaluate data, and revise menus, if needed.
8. Create reports.

Chapter 2:

The Dietary Specifications

CHAPTER OBJECTIVES

After reading this chapter, you will understand how to:

1. Discuss Dietary Specifications requirements for school meals.
2. Explain Dietary Specifications requirements related to USDA-defined age/grade groups.

A dietary specification is the required level of calories, saturated fat, *trans* fat, or sodium for a specific age/grade group. The Dietary Specifications were established to serve as a measure of the nutritional quality of school meals.

Regulations require that breakfast and/or lunch menus offered and averaged over a week meet the Dietary Specifications for the age/grade group for which they are intended. The Dietary Specifications for breakfast and lunch must be evaluated separately.

Four Dietary Specifications:

Weekly average requirements:

- Calories (range)
- Saturated Fat (maximum)
- Sodium (maximum)

Daily requirement restriction:

- *Trans* Fat (maximum)

For total calories, **minimums** and **maximums** are established by age/grade group and must be met on average over the school week. By keeping calories within the acceptable ranges, menu planners ensure adequate, consistent calorie levels to meet children's energy and development needs, while also reducing the risk of overconsumption.

> **HELPFUL TIP**
> Menu planners should select nutrient dense foods and ingredients, and avoid products that are high in fats, added sugars, and added sodium.

Pre-Publication Copy

In order to reduce *trans* fat, sodium, and the percentage of calories from saturated fat, the Dietary Specifications for these are **maximums**.

Food products and ingredients used <u>daily</u> must contain zero grams of *trans* fat per serving (naturally occurring *trans* fats are exempt). It is important to note *trans* fat will not be evaluated in the nutrient analysis, therefore the State agency must review nutrition labeling or manufacturer specifications for products or ingredients used to prepare school meals to verify they contain zero grams (less than 0.5 grams) of *trans* fat per serving.

Meeting a Child's Overall Nutrient Needs:

USDA recognizes that the Dietary Specifications do not include all the nutrients for which Dietary Reference Intakes (DRIs) have been established. The required meal pattern (components and quantities) ensures that children are offered foods that contain certain amounts vitamins and minerals required for optimal growth and development. Therefore, following the meal pattern requirements, and monitoring the nutrients for which Dietary Specifications have been established, should ensure that children's overall nutrient needs are met.

Nutrition research indicates that, for optimum health, humans need an array of biologically-active compounds that occur in a variety of foods (e.g., fruits, vegetables, whole grains). USDA is committed to the principle that school meals be comprised of an assortment of foods which provide naturally occurring nutrients, as recommended in the Dietary Guidelines, rather than formulated foods which have been artificially fortified.

Nutrition Standards for Meals

The meal patterns are designed to reflect different nutrient and calorie needs of students and accommodate the grade structure in the majority of schools. USDA has also established age/grade group-specific Dietary Specifications.

Required Age/Grade Groups for Meal Pattern: Breakfast and Lunch

* Grades K-5
* Grades 6-8
* Grades 9-12

Single Menu Allowable for Lunch K-8

If a K-8 school is unable to offer different meal patterns for grades K-5 and grades 6-8 students, the menu planner may offer students in these grades the same quantities of food components because the lunch meal pattern requirements for the K-5 and 6-8 age/grade groups narrowly overlap. However, the school district would have to be careful to meet the sodium and calorie requirements for each age/grade group. For example, if a single menu is offered to grades K-8, it must comply with the K-5 sodium requirement (also compliant with the grades 6-8 requirement); furthermore, average calories must be in the range where the K-5 and 6-8 requirements overlap (i.e., between 600-650 calories for lunch).

If one menu is served to K-8 students, a single nutrient analysis may be conducted for K-8, however it may be advantageous to run separate analyses if the nutrient analysis is not meeting the Dietary Specifications to determine where the menu may need to be adjusted.

Single Menu Allowable for Breakfast K-12

The same concept occurs with breakfast. There is overlap in the Dietary Specifications for all grade groups for breakfast; therefore it is possible to meet all the Dietary Specifications with one breakfast menu (K-12). A single weighted analysis may be conducted however the sodium and calorie requirements for each age/grade group must meet the overlap of all three age grade groups. For example a K-12 breakfast menu must provide between 450-500 calories and comply with the K-5 sodium requirements. It may be advantageous to run separate analyses for each age/grade group if the nutrient analysis is not meeting the Dietary Specifications to determine where the menu may need to be adjusted.

Chapter 3:

Key Nutrient Analysis Concepts

Overview of the Software Database
(including the Child Nutrition (CN) Database)

An accurate nutrient analysis is critical in assessing compliance with dietary specifications. In cooperation with the USDA's Agricultural Research Service (ARS), FNS developed the CN Database to provide accurate, reliable, and centralized nutrient data for analysis of school meals. All USDA-approved software includes the CN Database.

The **CN Database** contains the nutrient profiles of food items commonly used in SFAs/schools and contains nutrients that are monitored by the Child Nutrition Program.

The CN Database includes:

- Selected food items from the USDA Nutrient Database for Standard Reference;

- USDA foods;

- Nutrient profiles for USDA Recipes and Recipes for Healthy Kids;

- Many brand name commercially prepared foods provided by food industry; and

- Yield information from USDA's *Food Buying Guide for Child Nutrition Programs.*

These files are *locked*, which means the information in these files may be accessed and copied, but may not be altered by the local user.

Pre-Publication Copy

Database requirements for USDA-approved nutrient analysis software programs:

- Software must contain the most current version of the CN Database.

- The software may include brand name food items with nutrient data that has been supplied directly to the software vendors by food industry. The user must be able to differentiate between food industry items in the CN Database and food industry items added by the software developers.

- Foods and recipes added by the software vendor or by the user must have the source designated as "Local."

All Foods Are Included in the Nutrient Analysis

All food or menu items offered in a reimbursable meal, *including condiments/accompaniments*, are included in the nutrient analysis and count toward meeting the Dietary Specifications for the meal.

Schools may offer extra foods (e.g., ice cream, pudding) that do not credit toward any food component required in a reimbursable meal. Extra foods offered must be included in the nutrient analysis and count toward the limits on calories, saturated fat, sodium, and *trans* fat.

> **Are foods served to students with special needs included in the nutrient analysis?**
>
> 1. When food or menu item substitutions are made for students with special dietary needs, the meals are not included in the nutrient analysis.
> 2. If food or menu items served to students with special dietary needs are the same menu items served to the entire age/grade group, only modified for texture, the food or menu items are included in the nutrient analysis.

Foods that are considered *Foods of Minimal Nutritional Value* (FMNV) under 7 CFR Parts 210 and 220, Appendices B (i.e., chewing gum, soda water, water ices, and certain candies) are included in the nutrient analysis calculations only if they are used as a garnish in a menu item. For example, even though jelly beans are a food of FMNV, a menu planner would include them in the nutrient analysis if they are used as a cake decoration.

Appendix C provides more information on Foods of Minimal Nutritional Value. [**NOTE:** When Standards for All Foods Sold in School are implemented on July 1, 2014, the Foods of Minimal Nutritional Value category will be eliminated. For additional information, see the Smart Snacks Interim Final Rule at http://www.gpo.gov/fdsys/pkg/FR-2013-06-28/pdf/2013-15249.pdf.]

Only reimbursable meals are included in nutrient analyses. Therefore, adult meals and a la carte sales must not be included in nutrient analyses.

Pre-Publication Copy

Nutrients Calculated "As Consumed" or "Edible Form"

A nutrient analysis is conducted to calculate the nutrients in the finished food products as they will be consumed by students. It is important to note that recipes for nutrient analysis, including the ingredients used in the recipes, may be very different from the standardized recipe that the cook uses in food production. This is because many of the ingredients in a standardized food production or cook's recipe may be in the "as purchased" form such as raw ground beef, raw chopped onions and raw green pepper for a

> **YIELD FACTOR METHOD**
>
> A method for nutrient analysis of recipes that requires that each raw recipe ingredient be converted and entered in the recipe database as ready-to-serve or cooked. If the database does not include raw-to-cooked yield for a specific ingredient, use the yield data from USDA's *Food Buying Guide for Child Nutrition Programs* to convert from the raw to the cooked form.

meatloaf — which will then be prepared or cooked from scratch in the school kitchen(s). The nutrient content of foods may vary greatly depending on the method of preparation. As foods cook, they may lose moisture and nutrients. All ingredients in recipes prepared "from scratch" must be entered into the computer using the Yield Factor Method to account for the changes in nutrient values due to preparation and cooking.

The Yield Factor Method will be explained in more detail during the discussion of the procedures for entering recipes in Chapter 8.

Nutrients Averaged over the School Week

State agencies will monitor calories, saturated fat, and sodium in the meals served to students in grades K -12. Breakfast and lunch menus are analyzed over one school week within the review period. When evaluating the Dietary Specifications, state agencies may not combine breakfast and lunch analyses.

Definition of School Week

For the purposes of nutrient analysis, a school week represents a normal school week of five consecutive days. To accommodate weeks that are either shorter or longer than the five consecutive days, the analyzed week should contain a minimum of three consecutive days and a maximum of seven consecutive days. When school lunches are offered less than three times in a week, combine these menus with either the previous week's menus or the subsequent week's menus.

For example, during the week of Thanksgiving, an SFA/school serves lunch only two days that week. Those two days could be combined with either the week before or the week after Thanksgiving. The same situation might arise around other holiday periods or during the first and last weeks of school.

By combining a menu week that only has one or two days in it with another week, the school avoids problems in meeting the Dietary Specifications that can result from analyzing a small sample of meals.

Weighted Averages

National School Lunch Program (NSLP) and School Breakfast Program (SBP) regulations require *weighted averages* for conducting nutrient analyses. A weighted nutrient analysis gives more weight to nutrients in popular foods that are more frequently *selected* by students. Weighted analyses allows for a greater contribution of nutrients to come from menu items that are selected more often and less nutrient contribution from those menu items selected less often. More discussion of weighted averages will be provided in Chapter 9.

Whole Foods Versus Fortification

USDA is committed to the fundamental Dietary Guidelines premise that nutrients should come primarily from foods. Nutrient dense foods contain essential vitamins and minerals that are often contained in nutrient supplements, and also contain dietary fiber and other biologically active compounds (e.g., flavenoids, carotenoids, and other phytonutrients) that may have positive health effects.

Schools offering meals that contain a variety of nutrient dense foods, especially dark green red and orange vegetables; beans and peas; whole grains; and fat-free or low-fat milk and milk products, will meet Dietary Guidelines.

School meals also provide an opportunity to teach children about healthful eating. Learning to make food choices to nourish and optimize health is an important and valuable life skill. Consequently, it is essential for children to learn about, and recognize, foods and the variety of nutrients they provide.

Chapter 4

Selecting Software for Nutrient Analysis

CHAPTER OBJECTIVES

After reading this chapter, you will understand how to:
- Select software for nutrient analysis.
- Explain the various functions that USDA-approved software programs allow.
- Choose an approved nutrient analysis program.

USDA-Approved Nutrient Analysis Software Programs

USDA approves software to be used for the Administrative Review to ensure valid and consistent nutrient data.

- State agencies must use USDA-approved software when conducting a nutrient analysis.

- SFAs/schools conducting their own nutrient analysis must use USDA-approved software if they want the State agency to accept their nutrient analysis for the Administrative Review.

CN Database in Approved Software

To be eligible for USDA approval, the nutrient analysis software program must contain the current CN Database developed specifically for analysis of school meals. Software manufacturers are expected to update their software within 90 days of the date a new CN database version is released.

USDA-approved software programs allow you to:
- Enter the nutrient data of a new food item from a Nutrition Facts label or from a manufacturer's nutrient analysis data report.

Using Software with the Most Current CN Database

Federal guidelines require USDA-approved nutrient analysis software developers to update their customers with the most recent CN Database release to remain approved for use in Child Nutrition Programs. State agencies and SFAs are encouraged to work with their software vendor to ensure that they are using software with the most current CN Database version. Each revision contains updated nutrient data, new commercially prepared items, and USDA Foods nutrient information. A list of USDA-approved software is available on the Healthy Meals Resource System website: http://healthymeals.nal.usda.gov/menu-planning/nutrient-analysis-software-approved-usda/nutrient-analysis-software-approved-use.

- Enter, modify and analyze recipes.

- Plan, copy, or modify menus for a 3- to 7-day school week.

- Compare nutrient analysis of the weekly breakfast or lunch menu to a specific nutrient standard and indicate when standards are not being met.

- Search the database for food items containing specific nutrients in order to modify menus to meet the nutrient standard.

- Create reports, such as nutrient composition, menus, and recipe analysis.

A more detailed description of the software program requirements and functions is provided in Appendix D.

Choosing an Approved Nutrient Analysis Software Program

Differences in Software Programs

While the USDA-approved software programs must include the functions outlined in Appendix D, there are still many differences between the USDA-approved software programs.

- Some programs perform only nutrient analysis.

- Some programs are part of a larger system that include many other school foodservice software modules, such as Free and Reduced Price modules, Food Production modules, and Inventory modules.

- Operating system and hardware requirements vary.

The SFA/school and State agency will need to do some research to find the program that best meets the needs of your school district/school or State agency. Confer with your computer personnel to ensure software compatibility with existing hardware.

Questions to Consider When Selecting Software

- Do you need software that does only nutrient analysis, or do you want related program applications that perform many functions such as procurement, inventory, enhanced production records, etc.?

- Do you want a Windows-based system? A networked system?

Pre-Publication Copy

- What are the hardware requirements? Will current hardware support the software requirements? Check with your technology support team in the State agency or SFA for guidance.

- Are you able to participate in a demonstration of the software program at a conference or through other means?

- Can you visit a site that is using the software program in which you are interested?

- How easy is the program to use for entering data? Consider who will be using the program and staff computer literacy.

- How efficient is the overall nutrient analysis process? How well does the "search" feature help you locate food items (ingredients) and recipes in the database?

- Are reports easy to understand? Is it easy to interpret the results of the nutrient analysis and modify the recipes and menus to adjust results?

- How often is the software updated? Will the updates be provided as part of your initial cost or be separately priced? What are the update costs?

- What will the software package initially cost for one school/for the district? Consider how many copies or licenses for the software will be needed.

- What support is available? Online, telephone, on site? What does it cost?

> **NOTE:** USDA only reviews and monitors the CN Database and software functions that relate directly to nutrient analyses and meal pattern contributions. USDA does not review or approve other functions added by software vendors.

Chapter 5:
Overview of Conducting a Nutrient Analysis

CHAPTER OBJECTIVES

After reading this chapter, you will understand how to:
- Use the CN Database in conjunction with vendor-added and user-added data.
- List the five steps needed to conduct a nutrient analysis.

The exact steps to conducting a nutrient analysis may vary slightly among software programs, but there are similar functions. Menu planners and State agency staff must understand and carefully follow the procedures or protocols for each step to conduct an accurate nutrient analysis, regardless of the software program.

Detailed descriptions of each step will be provided in the following chapters but initially the user must understand several principles or concepts prior to conducting a nutrient analysis.

Before beginning the process of entering new food items into the nutrient analysis software database, the user should understand how the software database has been developed.

Contents of the Nutrient Analysis Software Database

There are two parts to the software database:

1. Child Nutrition (CN) Database

All USDA-approved nutrient analysis software programs must contain the most current version of the CN Database. All files in the CN Database are *locked* which means they cannot be modified or deleted by the user. The CN Database includes:

> The USDA-approved nutrient analysis software contains foods or ingredients in the CN Database and also allows the user to add, modify, and delete food or ingredient items and recipes in the local database.

- **USDA Standard Reference Foods or Ingredients:** The CN Database contains foods or ingredients most commonly used in school meals from the USDA Nutrient Database for Standard Reference. These foods or ingredients are identified in the software database under the Source as **USDA Nutrient Database**.

- **Commercially Prepared Foods:** FNS contracts with a private company to manage the CN Database. Because SFAs/schools use numerous commercially prepared products,

Pre-Publication Copy

manufacturers are encouraged to submit nutritional information for their products so they can be added to the CN Database. This saves data entry time for local school districts/schools and State agencies and makes nutritional information on those products available nationwide. A sample of the form to be completed by manufacturers for submission of data is included in Appendix F. These food products or ingredients are identified in the software database under the Source as **Food Industry**.

- **USDA Foods:** The CN Database contains the current USDA foods available to school districts/schools. These food products or ingredients are identified in the software database under the Source as **USDA Foods**. The CN Database does not include USDA Foods that are processed under State processing contracts. For more information about USDA Foods, see http://www.fns.usda.gov/fdd/foods/healthy/ToolKit.htm.

- **USDA *Food Buying Guide* Yield Data:** The CN Database contains yield data from the *Food Buying Guide* as a tool to assist the menu planner in determining raw-to-cooked yields for recipe analysis. It also provides yield data for many other foods from an as purchased form (AP) to the edible portion (EP) of the food. This yield data is also useful for volume/weight conversions from the purchase unit, e.g., can size to cups, cups per pound, and cans to weight.

- **USDA Recipes and Recipes for Healthy Kids:** The CN Database contains all current USDA-standardized quantity recipes for school foodservice. Only the nutrient information is included — not the recipe ingredients and directions. If a school uses the USDA recipe exactly as displayed on the recipe card (first listed ingredient when alternates are listed and no optional ingredients), the nutrient analysis for the USDA quantity recipes in the CN Database is the most accurate selection for menu analysis. Some software companies have entered the USDA standardized quantity recipes into a separate recipe database, with each ingredient listed, to make it easier for school districts/schools to modify the recipes. USDA Recipes for Schools are available at: http://www.fns.usda.gov/tn/Resources/usda_recipes.html. Recipes for Healthy Kids are available at: http://teamnutrition.usda.gov/Resources/r4hk_schools.html.

> **Companies that want their products entered into the CN Database** should visit the Healthy School Meals Resource System website at: http://healthymeals.nal.usda.gov/online-web-tool-submitting-nutrient-data-0

2. Local Database

In addition to the CN Database, some software manufacturers include nutrient data in their local databases for the following:

- Commercially prepared products, and

Pre-Publication Copy

- Raw-to-cooked yield data for certain products

These vendor-added commercially prepared food products or ingredients are identified in the software database under the Source as **Local.**

All USDA-approved software also allows the user to:

- Enter the nutrient data for new food items, and

- Enter, modify, and analyze recipes.

These user-added or modified food products and recipes should be identified in the software database under the Source as **Local.**

Overview of Steps for Conducting a Nutrient Analysis

STEP 1
Preparing for Nutrient Analysis – Gathering the Materials

This process will be discussed in-depth in Chapter 6. Materials include:

- Breakfast and lunch menus including menu choices and portion sizes for each age/grade group and menu type.

- Standardized recipes, including USDA Recipes and local recipes that will be used in the menus.

- Description or specifications for all food products used in the menus.

- Nutrient information for ingredients used in recipes that are not included in the software database,

- Food production records to assist in weighting the more frequently selected items and document if reimbursable meals were offered to students. If this is an entirely new set of menus this information may not be available until the menus for an entire menu cycle have been served.

STEP 2
Entering Food Items (Ingredients) into the Local Database

Pre-Publication Copy

This process will be discussed further in Chapter 7 and includes:

- Reviewing the recipes to be used in the cycle menus (SFA) or the review week's menus for the school (State agency) and identifying ingredients missing in the software database.

- Entering the missing ingredients, including volume and weight measurements, and nutrient information.

How Food Manufacturers Provide Nutrient Information

Manufacturers provide nutrient analysis information in one of two ways — **as purchased** or **as served.**

- **As purchased** nutrient analysis data represents the nutritional content of a weight and/or a volume or other measurable amount of the product *exactly as it is purchased*; that is, the nutrients contained in a certain amount of an **unprepared** cornbread mix or an **unbaked** prepared whole grain pizza or pre-fried egg roll. Note: "The Nutrition Facts" labels on products are required to provide "as purchased" data. A sample copy of a Nutrition Facts Label is included in Appendix E.

- **As served** nutrient analysis data provides the nutrient values for a product *after it has been further prepared*. For example, cornbread mix will provide as purchased data on the unprepared mix and may also provide as served data on the mix when prepared according to package instructions.

Food Products Used "As Purchased"

For **ready-to-serve** products, i.e., foods that only require chilling, heating and/or portioning and are used as purchased, use the nutrient data exactly as provided on the food product and enter it into the ingredient database.

> **HELPFUL TIP**
> When entering new ingredients, always indicate whether the nutrient data is "as purchased" or "as served," and indicate the cooking method.

Food Products Prepared According to Manufacturer's "As Served" Nutrient Information

When a manufacturer provides as served nutrient analysis information, specifies the cooking method, and the school foodservice prepares the food *exactly* according to directions, use the nutrient data exactly as provided on the food product and enter it into the ingredient database.

Food Products Requiring Further Preparation

For purchased products that do require further preparation, if the manufacturer *has not* provided "as served" nutrient information, or the SFA uses a differing preparation method, the user must develop a recipe for this prepared ingredient. This will be further described in Chapter 8.

Pre-Publication Copy

STEP 3
Adding Recipes to the Local Database

Select the correct food items from the database for each recipe in the menus. The person who adds recipes to the software for the nutrient analysis must have knowledge of the foods that are purchased and how they will be prepared and served in order to select the correct item for the recipes. The software, including the CN Database, contains multiple entries (and different nutrient content) of the same food item, based on the varieties, types, and forms of the food item and different preparation methods.

Recipes are nutritionally analyzed based on the form in which the food is consumed. If quantity recipes include raw ingredients that will be cooked or further prepared before consuming, they will need conversion to the *edible* form of the ingredient. This is referred to as the Yield Factor Method and will be further discussed in Chapter 8.

Basic Rules for the Yield Factor Method

- Use the form and portion of the food as offered.

- Select raw if not heated or cooked.

- Select cooked (or a cooked preparation method) if cooked before serving, using the database food code for the cooked ingredient.

Convert or adjust the amount of the raw ingredient in the recipe by using a yield factor from the *Food Buying Guide*. Some commonly used cooked food products in schools have a raw-to-cooked conversion factor included in the software. If this option is available, it will eliminate the need to convert the raw weight to the cooked yield.

> **What is the Yield Factor Method?**
>
> Yield Factor Method is a method for nutrient analysis of recipes that requires that each raw ingredient be converted and entered into the recipe database as ready-to-serve or cooked.
>
> If the database does not include raw-to-cooked yield information for a specific ingredient, use yield data from USDA's *Food Buying Guide for Child Nutrition Programs* to convert from the raw to the cooked form.

STEP 4
Entering Specific Menu Planning Data

The order of this process may differ between software programs, but the data needed to complete the nutrient analysis is common among programs.

- Identify menu name(s) or site names and associated age/grade group for each menu type offered.

Pre-Publication Copy

- Identify menu or meal type, such as breakfast or lunch.

- Develop individual menus or link to cycle menus.

- Assign dates to menus and determine a date range for each nutrient analysis, as defined by the school week.

- Determine the number of servings of reimbursable meals and the serving sizes of food or menu items.

- Create the reports for review.

STEP 5
Evaluating and Modifying Menus and Recipes to Comply with Dietary Specifications Requirements

- Review menus for variety.

- Review the weekly nutrient analyses, noting Dietary Specifications that have not been met.

- If necessary, modify the menus to meet the Dietary Specifications.

- Reanalyze menus when menus/food items change, products change, recipes change, or when participation or student selections change.

Chapter 6:

Preparing for a Nutrient Analysis

> **CHAPTER OBJECTIVES**
>
> **After reading this chapter, you will understand how to:**
> - Collect the necessary materials and information for conducting a nutrient analysis.
> - Collect nutrient data or information for food items that are not listed in the CN Database.

Information and Materials Needed for Nutrient Analyses

Whether you are an SFA conducting your own analysis, or a State agency conducting analysis during an Administrative Review, you will need to have the following materials ready and available to conduct an accurate nutrient analysis.

1. Menus

When the State agency conducts a nutrient analysis as part of an Administrative Review of an SFA, State staff will choose one week within the review period to evaluate the dietary specifications for breakfast and lunch at the selected school. The site is selected based on results from the *Meal Compliance Risk Assessment Tool*. The State agency will collect the menu documentation for each USDA established age/grade group and menu types offered at breakfast and lunch and conduct a weighted nutrient analysis of all menu and food items, including condiments, offered as part of the reimbursable meal. In other words, a separate nutrient analysis is required for each age/grade group at the selected review site and if the review site has different menu offerings for different segments of students in the school, separate analyses are required for each population segment.

Example:

A school serving 6-12 graders plans two different lunch menus, one menu for 6-8 and another menu for 9-12. In this case, the school is offering two different lunch menus for different segments of students in the school. The SA will need to conduct two weighted nutrient analyses for lunch: one for the 6-8th grade students and one for 9-12th grade students to ensure each menu type meets the dietary specifications.

If the SFA or school district is conducting its own nutrient analysis of menus — the SFA will need a complete set of draft or tentative menus prepared for data entry. Written menus should

Pre-Publication Copy

include all menu or food choices with portion sizes to be served to each USDA established grade/age groupings and menu type for breakfast and lunch.

Most SFAs plan *centralized cycle menus*. School districts that conduct nutrient analyses find that cycle menus, repeated on a periodic basis, save time and resources. For purposes of the Administrative Review, nutrient analyses must be for the targeted menu review site only, not a SFA-wide nutrient analysis.

2. Standardized Recipes

In order to ensure that the nutrient analysis reflects what is offered, all schools **must** use standardized recipes. Standardized recipes are those that have been tried and tested and found to be acceptable to students, have the same ingredients and method of preparation, and provide a consistent yield.

Standardized recipes should be available for input into the nutrient analysis software or be available to provide to the State agency during an Administrative Review.

3. Food Product Descriptions or Specifications

The school district should have written food product descriptions or specifications for all foods used in the schools — not only as a purchasing tool but also for determining which product or ingredient to select from the software for the analysis.

School districts that use procurement software can provide food product descriptions for each food product. This allows the school district/school menu planner or State agency staff to select the correct ingredient from the software database when conducting nutrient analysis.

> Examples of Food Product Descriptions:
>
> - Ground beef, frozen, no more than 20% fat
> - Milk, unflavored, 1% low-fat

4. Nutrient Data or Information for Food Products Not in the Database

Identify food products not in the CN Database or in your software's local database.

- Review menus and the standardized recipes to be used for the preparation of the menus.

- Compare to the software to determine if all food items or ingredients are included.

For *single ingredient* foods or foods in the USDA *Food Buying Guide*, the nutrient data for most products will already be in the CN Database. Examples of single ingredient foods are fruits, vegetables, and milk.

For food products with more than one ingredient; the food may be in the CN Database or it may not, depending upon whether the food has a standard of identity or the product manufacturer has submitted the product information for inclusion in the CN Database. Some software manufacturers also include a limited number of commercially prepared products in their ingredient database. These will be labeled as Local.

- If the product is not in the CN Database or your software's local database, you will need to locate the nutrient information for the product.

- Sources of nutrient data other than CN Database are:
    o Nutrition Facts Labels, often found on institutional-sized product packaging, even though they are not required. A sample Nutrition Facts Label is shown in Appendix E.
    o Nutrient data provided by the manufacturer. A nutrient analysis data form you can ask the manufacturer to complete is included in Appendix F.
    o Nutrient analysis data from another reliable source, such as USDA's Nutrient Database for Standard Reference, available at: http://ndb.nal.usda.gov/

5. Food Production Records

All SFAs/schools are required to document the foods served to students as part of a reimbursable meal. In addition to ensuring that meals served adhere to meal requirements, production records also provide valuable information for conducting nutrient analyses of foods offered to children.

Food production records must include:

- Number of reimbursable meals planned, offered, and actually served;

- All menu items (or food items) planned, offered, and served for reimbursable meals including milk type(s) and condiments/accompaniments;

- Portion or serving sizes for each age/grade group;

- Recipes used (note if USDA recipe, or local recipe);

- Brand names, CN label numbers (if desired), and identification numbers of commercially prepared food products;

- Total amounts of foods planned, offered, and actually selected/served;

- Documentation of a la carte, adult, and/or other non-reimbursable meals, including number of portions for each of these food items; and

- Documentation of substitutions and/or leftovers used.

Planned, Offered & Selected/Served: what's the difference?

Planned: A planned menu is what the menu planner intends to offer to students.

Offered: An offered menu is what is actually prepared and set out on the line(s) for students. Offered menus may differ from "planned" menus because, for example, a planned food item was not received and the menu planner had to offer a different food item.

Selected/Served: Selected refers to which food items were actually taken by students.

A Menu Planner for Healthy School Meals (revised edition forthcoming) provides more information on documenting food production records and provides several sample food production record forms. Additionally, many State agencies have developed State prototypes or sample food production records for use by school districts/schools within the State. Several foodservice software companies—including companies that have approved nutrient analysis software—have software applications that can be used for creating computerized school-level food production records.

Chapter 7:
Entering Food Items (Ingredients) into the Local Database

CHAPTER OBJECTIVES

After reading this chapter, you will understand how to:
- Enter food items/ingredients into the local database, step-by-step.
- Delete and modify ingredients in the local database.

How to Enter Data for New Food Products or Ingredients

By this time, all of the recipes and food items or ingredients to be used in the nutrient analysis should have been identified.

Unless the food product description found in the CN Database or local software database **exactly matches** the food item your SFA/school is using, you'll need to create a new entry for each food item or ingredient using the nutrient data you obtained, and save it in the SFA local database.

Steps for entering new food items/ingredients into the software database:

Follow directions provided by your software program to add a food item or ingredient. The following are general steps to enter a new food item or ingredient.

STEP 1
Assign each new food product an identification number

Some software applications allow the user to assign an identification number while others assign identification numbers automatically. Some software also marks locally entered food items with a specific code. Enter an identification number for the new food item/ingredient or use the number assigned by your software.

HELPFUL TIP
Some State agency staff and SFAs find it helpful to write the database identification code number next to each ingredient on the copied standardized recipes. This helps identify ingredients that are missing in the database and reduces data entry time.

STEP 2
Enter a description of the food item/ingredient

Give the food item/ingredient a basic name and then add a short description that will help you locate and identify this food item/ingredient in the future (e.g., fully-cooked, frozen, raw). Some people find it helpful to include the brand name in the description.

STEP 3
Enter a food category for the food item/ingredient

Assigning a food category makes it easier to conduct a search for the food items.

STEP 4
Identify the source of the data as "Local."

For any food item entered by the local user, the source is always identified as "Local."

STEP 5
If the product is commercially prepared, enter the name of the manufacturer and/or brand name.

The brand name of a commercially prepared product can be very important in ensuring that the correct food item/ingredient is chosen from the database.

STEP 6
Enter the unit(s) of measurement for the food item/ingredient.

Add weight measure(s) for all different sized portions and/or weight/volume measures, if appropriate. It is important that the user enter correct measurement information from the label or other document, as all conversions are based on this entry(s). For items served by volume, a weight/volume relationship must be established. To perform a nutrient analysis of a certain volume of fruit and/or vegetable, you must enter a volume measure and the weight associated with that volume.

KEY POINT

The software cannot calculate the nutrient analysis of a volume measure unless the weight of a volume measure (e.g., teaspoon, tablespoon, cup) is provided by the user.

Refer to the product information from the Nutrition Facts Label/manufacturer's nutrient data information, the *Food Buying Guide* and other resources3 that will allow you to determine the serving size description, in weight, and if appropriate, corresponding volume.

Adding Food Items or Ingredients to Your Database

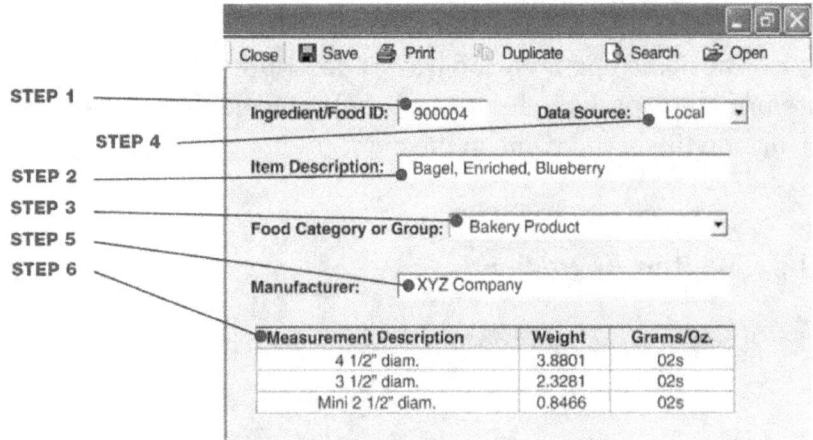

STEP 7
Enter the nutrient composition information

- Enter the base weight (the weight of the food item/ingredient for which the nutrient data has been provided). The base weight/nutrient content can be found on the Nutrition Facts Label or the manufacturer's nutrient data statement.

- Enter the serving size description associated with the base weight (oz, cup, each).

Other Helpful Resources:

- Bowes and Church, *Food Values of Portions Commonly Used*
- Molt, *Food for Fifty*
- USDA, Nutrient Database for Standard Reference, available at: http://ndb.nal.usda.gov/

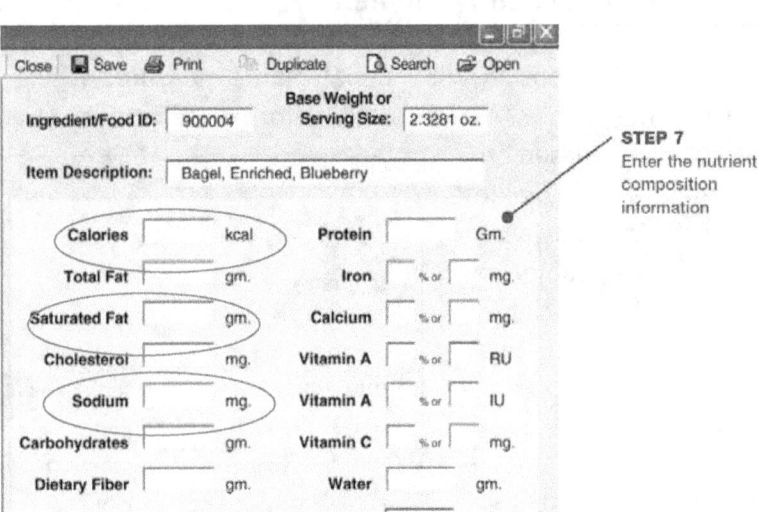

- Enter the actual values for calories, saturated fat, and sodium for the base weight.

- If the Nutrition Facts Label or the manufacturer's nutrient data statement indicates there is an insignificant amount of a nutrient, enter zero "O" for the nutrient value.

- It is not necessary to enter the information for water or ash for nutrient analysis; however, if the information is available, it provides a more accurate analysis of the product's weight.

KEY POINT

If there is no information for a required nutrient, follow the software directions to mark it as missing nutrient information. Do not enter zero "0" for missing nutrient information because:

1. You will not be able to identify missing data, and
2. The nutrient analysis will be inaccurate.

STEP 8
Review data entry for accuracy and save the data

Before saving the data, review each entry to ensure that the data has been entered correctly. Follow your software instructions for saving entered data.

STEP 9
Create a report of ingredients and recheck for accuracy

Most of the software programs allow the user to print the food item/ingredient information in various ways — alphabetically, by local food items/ingredients only, by food items/ingredients used in recipes only, and by missing nutrient data. This is a good way to check the accuracy of the data entry and to identify food items/ingredients with missing data.

To modify or delete ingredients, you must be in the modify/edit mode

Only food items entered by the local user in the local database may be modified or deleted.
- To modify an existing ingredient in the local database
    - Locate the product in the database, and
    - Repeat steps 2 through 7.

- To delete or deactivate a local food product from the database, follow the software instructions for deleting food products.

Chapter 8:
Adding a Recipe to the Local Database

CHAPTER OBJECTIVES

After reading this chapter, you will understand how to:
- Select the correct food items and correct measures of foods for recipes.
- Determine the difference between cook's recipes and recipes for nutrient analysis.
- Describe the Yield Factor Method using the *Food Buying Guide* when analyzing a recipe's nutrient content.
- Adjust moisture and fat loss or gain in selected commercially prepared products.

How the Nutrient Analyses of USDA Recipes Were Calculated

As discussed earlier, for USDA recipes, only the *nutrients, not the production recipes,* are included in the CN Database and the approved nutrient analysis software. It is important for the menu planner to understand the protocols used to analyze these recipes.

- **Based on first ingredient only.** When USDA recipes show alternate ingredient choices, the nutrient analysis is based on the first ingredient listed, not the alternate ingredient.

For example:

Recipe D-13 Beef or Pork Taco

Raw ground beef or raw ground pork is listed as an ingredient. The nutrient analysis in the CN Database is based on the first ingredient listed, raw ground beef. Therefore, if the SFA/school uses raw ground pork, or a combination of ground beef and ground turkey to prepare this recipe, a new recipe must be entered in the software or the recipe may be copied into a local recipe and edited. It is important that the recipe be entered as it is prepared so the nutrient analysis is accurate.

- **Optional ingredients are not included.** The nutrient analysis in the CN Database does not include any ingredients listed as optional in the recipe.

For example:

Recipe D-20 Chili Con Carne with Beans

Cheddar cheese is an optional ingredient in this recipe and was not included in the nutrient analysis. If cheddar cheese is included as an ingredient in the recipe, the recipe including cheddar cheese must be entered into the local recipe software database and the nutrient analysis recalculated. The user may also copy the existing recipe and edit accordingly to reflect the ingredients actually used.

- **Variations of some, but not all USDA Recipes are included in the CN Database.**

For example:

Recipe B-4 Baking Powder Biscuits

Four variations are included:

1. B-4a Baking Powder Biscuit using Master Mix

2. B-4b Cheese Biscuits

3. B-4c Drop Biscuits

4. B-4d Wheat Biscuits

If the school district/school is using a variation of a recipe that is not in the software, a new recipe with the recipe variation must be entered into the local software database and the nutrient analysis recalculated.

KEY POINT

Some software companies enter the USDA recipes as production (cook's) recipes, including ingredients, into the local database of their approved nutrient analysis software. This data entry may help schools easily modify the recipe for variations using alternate, optional, or unique ingredients. The user can simply copy and edit the recipe, instead of entering the entire recipe with the alternate ingredient or variation. State agencies and SFAs must review these recipes to ensure they have been entered according to nutrient analysis protocols, including yield factors. Some approved nutrient analysis software programs have functionality that allows the yield factors to be incorporated into the recipe. The recipes may lead to an inaccurate analysis after it is copied, unless it is edited by the user. Your software developer can help you follow their instructions for correctly entering recipes to result in an accurate nutrient analysis.

Selecting the Correct Food Items/Ingredients for Recipes

To ensure the correct calorie and nutritive value of the recipe, it is important to select the correct food item/ingredient from the software database. The nutrient content of raw foods is different from the nutrient content of cooked foods.

Recipes that require cooking are a challenge for nutrient analysis because the recipes contain raw ingredients, and yet we eat cooked products. Cooking changes the nutrient content, the moisture content, and, very frequently, the fat content.

Cooks' or Production Recipes Versus Recipes for Nutrient Analysis

Important: Recipes for nutrient analysis and cooks' or production recipes are usually **different.**

- The amount of calories and nutrients in a food will vary depending on the **edible portion** of the food and whether the food is raw or cooked.
- The ingredients in your standardized recipes or cooks' recipes usually indicate foods in their raw form, as purchased, including peel, bone, skin, etc.
- **For nutrient analysis purposes, recipes must include only the edible portion of a food.**
- Thus, the ingredient information in recipes must be adjusted or converted to reflect what is actually consumed.

KEY POINT

Individuals performing nutrient analyses must have knowledge of the foods that are purchased, and how they will be prepared and offered, to select the correct database item. The CN Database contains multiple entries (and nutrient content profiles) of the same food item, based on the varieties, types, and forms of the food item and different preparation methods.

Using the Yield Factor Method

After selecting the correct ingredient for the recipe, the SFA/State agency will need to use the Yield Factor Method to convert the raw, frozen, condensed, or dehydrated food item to the form the item will be when consumed. There are numerous food items or ingredients that need to be converted to an edible version such as raw meats, raw and frozen vegetables, and dried pasta that will be cooked before consumption.

Heat affects the nutrient content of many foods. The nutrient profiles of database foods described as cooked have been adjusted for the nutrient changes that occur with cooking. For example, the nutritive value of frozen green beans cooked with salt will be different from the nutritive value of canned green beans, which have been heated.

The Database features a list of nutritive values of foods prepared by various cooking methods. Cooked foods may be listed, for example, as:

- Boiled
- Broiled
- Baked
- Fried

 **KEY POINT**

The Yield Factor Method requires that each raw recipe ingredient be converted and entered in the recipe database as ready-to-serve or cooked. If the database does not have the raw-to-cooked yield for a specific ingredient, use yield data from USDA's *Food Buying Guide* to convert from the raw to the cooked form.

Vegetables

Vegetables that are indicated in the recipe in the as *raw* or *frozen* form will need to be converted to the *cooked* form because of change in nutrient and in the moisture content upon heating.

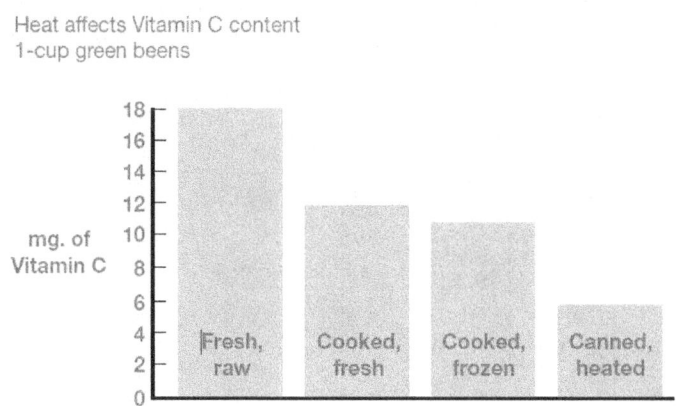

Nutrient Retention

Heat affects Vitamin C content
1-cup green beens

Example: Recipe Using Frozen Whole Green Beans

A recipe calls for 10 pounds of frozen whole green beans to be used to make Green Bean Casserole. To enter the recipe, you would select the cooked green beans (without salt) from the database. We selected *Beans, Green, Whole, Frozen, Boiled, No Salt* (CN Database #11061).

Pre-Publication Copy

- To convert the green beans, as purchased, to an edible amount of cooked green beans for the nutrient analysis, refer to the *Food Buying Guide*, page 2-8.

Section 2 – Vegetables (All Vegetable Subgroups)

1. Food As Purchased, AP	2. Purchase Unit	3. Servings Per Purchase Unit, EP	4. Serving Size per Meal Contribution	5. Purchase Units for 100 Servings	6. Additional Information
BEANS, GREEN – Other Subgroup (continued)					
Beans, Green, canned *Whole Includes USDA Foods*	Pound	8.20	1/4 cup drained vegetable	12.2	
Beans, Green, frozen *Cut Includes USDA Foods*	Pound	11.60	1/4 cup cooked, drained vegetable	8.7	
Beans, Green, frozen *French style Includes USDA Foods*	Pound	12.00	1/4 cup cooked, drained vegetable	8.4	
Beans, Green, frozen *Whole Includes USDA Foods*	Pound	10.70	1/4 cup cooked, drained vegetable	9.4	1 lb AP = 0.88 lb (about 2-5/8 cups) cooked drained vegetable
BEANS, GREEN, FLAT ITALIAN - Other Subgroup					
Beans, Green, Flat Italian, canned *Whole*	No. 10 can (103 oz)	35.10	1/4 cup heated, drained vegetable	2.9	1 No. 10 can = about 56.6 oz (8-3/4 cups) heated, drained beans
	No. 10 can (103 oz)	42.70	1/4 cup drained vegetable	2.4	1 No. 10 can = about 63.3 oz (10-5/8 cups) drained, unheated beans
Beans, Green, Flat Italian, frozen *Whole*	Pound	9.30	1/4 cup cooked, drained vegetable	10.8	1 lb AP = 0.91 lb (about 2-1/4 cups) cooked, drained beans

> NOTE: The yield and nutritive value differences are small between "heated" and "unheated" canned food items, so menu planners may use the data for "unheated" canned food items for nutrient analysis.

- The *Food Buying Guide* indicates that each pound of frozen green beans yields 0.88 pounds of cooked, drained green beans.

  10 pounds X 0.88 = 8.8 pounds of cooked green beans

Pre-Publication Copy

- The menu planner would select CN database, number 11061, *Beans, Green, Whole, Frozen, Boiled, No Salt* and enter a weight of 8.8 pounds of cooked green beans into the Green Bean Casserole recipe.

Fresh Vegetables in Cooked Recipes

There are several fresh vegetables that are frequently added to school recipes made from scratch. To expedite the conversion of these vegetables from raw-to-cooked, conversion from yield data in the *Food Buying Guide* of 1 pound raw-to-cooked is provided in Appendix G.

Meats

There are a number of factors that must be considered in entering recipes that contain raw meat for nutrient analysis. Remember, the recipe must be analyzed to reflect the nutrients in the recipe that the children will actually consume (Yield Factor Method).

When there is "Raw-to-cooked yield" in the database:

Several of the meat items in the software database have a conversion factor built in for raw-to-cooked data. For those items, the computer will calculate the nutritive value of the cooked yield when the amount of raw meat in the recipe is entered.

KEY POINT

The Yield Factor Method uses cooked ingredients for raw foods in recipes that are cooked, and adjusting the amount of ingredient in the recipe by using yield data from the approved software program, or USDA's *Food Buying Guide*. The "cooked codes" and cooked yields will reflect the losses or gains in moisture and fat, and the effect of cooking on other nutrients.

When raw-to-cooked data is available, a user would:

1. Select the "cooked" meat item from the database,

2. Select yield after cooking, raw-to-cooked, raw, raw yields, or other language used by your software program that indicates you may enter a raw weight,

3. Enter the weight of the raw meat as indicated in the recipe, and

4. The analysis will be calculated by the software using the nutritive values and cooked weight conversion from raw weight.

When there is no "raw-to-cooked yield" in the database:

What if the software does not indicate that you can enter the raw weight of the meat? In that case, you must convert the raw weight in the recipe to the cooked or edible weight, using the Yield Factor Method.

Pre-Publication Copy

To convert raw weight to edible or cooked weight, a user would:

1. Select the cooked meat item from the database,

2. Convert the raw weight to the edible or cooked weight by multiplying the raw weight of the meat called for in the recipe by the percent yield in the *Food Buying Guide* (Column 6)

3. Enter the cooked weight into the computer

Example of converting raw-to-cooked yield for Beef Stew:

Recipe for Beef Stew
An SFA/school is serving a recipe for beef stew which calls for 21 lbs. of raw stew meat (the recipe calls for browning the meat and draining the fat) and there is no raw-to-cooked yield for beef stew in their database. For the nutrient analysis, staff would check the USDA *Food Buying Guide* for the cooked yield of stew meat (61 percent), calculate the cooked weight, and enter that figure along with the cooked item for, stew meat, such as CN Database item would be #23090, *Beef, Chuck for Stew, separable lean and fat*. This example is shown below:

To correctly enter this recipe for nutrient analysis, the user would enter the correct identification code for cooked beef stew meat (23090) or find cooked beef stew meat through the search feature. Then enter 12.81 pounds.

Converting Raw Weight of Beef Stew Meat to Cooked Weight
Example
Your recipe calls for 21 lbs. of raw beef stew meat. You need to know the weight of the stew meat after cooking. Information excerpted from the USDA *Food Buying Guide*.

Food as Purchased	Beef, Stew Meat (composite of trimmed retail cuts)
Purchase Unit	Pound
Additional yield information	1 lb. "As Purchased" = .61 lbs. cooked lean meat

Answer: 21 lbs. x .61 = 12.81 lbs. of cooked beef stew meat

"As Purchased" vs. "Edible Portion" of Chicken (without bones and or skin)

The nutritive value of a three-ounce portion of cooked chicken with the skin and bones will be different from the nutritive value of a three-ounce portion of cooked boneless chicken.

If a recipe calls for 25 lbs of raw chicken thighs to be baked and served with the skin, you must convert the 25 lbs. of **as purchased** raw chicken thighs to the equivalent weight of the baked meat and skin only.

To enter the correct chicken ingredient into the recipe, select CN Database # 5094, *Chicken, Thigh, Roasted, with Skin*, and enter: 13 pounds.

The *Food Buying Guide* also contains **as purchased** to **edible portion** yield data for cooked chicken without skin.

Example of Converting Raw Chicken to Cooked Chicken with Skin

Your recipe calls for 25 lbs. of raw chicken thighs. You need to know the weight of the edible portion of the cooked chicken meat with skin (without the bones).

Food as Purchased	Chicken thigh, 4 oz.
Purchase Unit	Pound
Additional yield information	1 lb. "As Purchased" = .52 lbs. cooked chicken with skin

Answer: 25 lbs. x .52 = 13 lbs. of cooked chicken with skin

Exception to Use of Yield Factor Method for Some Cooked Meats

There is an exception to the rule of choosing a cooked meat item from the database and calculating the cooked meat yield. When you are entering a recipe where the fat will remain in the final product, you must select the raw meat database item and enter the weight of the raw meat into the recipe for analysis.

For example, if you are analyzing a recipe for Red Beans with Sausage, and the recipe instructions specify to slice the uncooked sausage and add it to the beans during cooking, you need to select the raw sausage data and the weight of the raw product. This is because the fat which would normally have cooked out and been drained off will remain in the final product. (This is a good example of a recipe that should be modified using either the cooking method and/or ingredients, to reduce saturated fat.)

Other examples of situations where you would choose the raw meat database item and enter the weight of the raw meat into the recipe for analysis include recipes for soups or stews where raw meat is added to the soup or stew and the fat contained in the raw meat ends up in the final product. However, if the soup or stew is chilled after preparation and the fat is skimmed off the top, it is appropriate to choose the cooked meat item from the database and enter the cooked weight of the meat.

Dried Pasta
Determining Cooked Volume of Dried Pasta

A recipe for Spaghetti and Marinara Sauce calls for cooking the dried pasta in boiling salted water prior to combining it with the sauce. This presents a difficult situation for nutrient analysis because the pasta does not absorb the total amount of either the boiling water or the salt during cooking. This problem can be resolved by selecting Spaghetti, Cooked, Enriched, with Added Salt from the CN Database, item number 20321. But first, the weight of the dried pasta has to be converted to the appropriate amount of cooked pasta, using the Yield Factor Method. The water and salt used in the recipe are **not included** in the computer data entry for the nutrient analysis.

The user would select the *Spaghetti, Cooked, Enriched, with Added Salt* from the CN Database (#20321) and enter: 21 cups of cooked spaghetti.

Example of Converting Dried Weight of Spaghetti to Cooked Volume

Determining cooked volume of 4 lbs. of dried spaghetti from the USDA *Food Buying Guide*

Food as Purchased	Dried Spaghetti
Purchase Unit	Pound
Servings per purchase unit	10.6
Serving size or portion	1/2 cup

Answer: Yield data from *Food Buying Guide* indicates 1 lb. dried spaghetti = 5.25 cups cooked pasta
4 lbs. x 5.25 cups = 21 cups of cooked spaghetti

Exception: If the **pasta is cooked in and absorbs recipe liquid**, the dry pasta would be the appropriate item to select and the dry weight of the pasta would be entered. For example, a recipe for Lasagna with Ground Beef calls for the lasagna noodles to be cooked in the tomato sauce. In this case, dried lasagna noodles would be the selected and the dry weight of the noodles called for in the recipe would be entered.

Adjusting Moisture and Fat Loss or Gain in Commercially Prepared Food Products

Many commercially prepared food products, such as frozen French fries, chicken nuggets, and fish portions, will undergo further preparation in the school kitchen.

The most common preparation technique is oven heating (bringing a fully-cooked product to the proper serving temperature). Because oven heating generally has minimal impact on moisture or fat loss, fully cooked, prepared food products that are only oven heated do not need adjustment for fat/moisture loss. However, these same products may have significant moisture loss and fat gain during deep-frying.

Although healthier preparation methods are encouraged, software already contains some fried food items that reflect moisture loss and fat gains which occur during deep frying. For example, if an SFA uses generic frozen French fried potatoes and deep-fat fries them in commodity vegetable oil, the best selection from the CN Database would be Item 50491, *Potatoes, French-fried, with salt, oven heated.*

Users may select this existing item rather than entering data on the French fries you are purchasing and adjusting for moisture loss and fat gain, since this item description already reflects moisture loss and fat absorption.

HELPFUL TIP
Always check the software first and use the item that reflects the cooking method for the food item.

However, there are commercially prepared products that **may not be available in the software** as a deep-fried version. If you serve a commercially prepared product which will be deep fried, and it is not in the database, you will need to create a recipe that can be adjusted for moisture losses and fat gains which occur with frying (unless the Nutrition Facts Label or the manufacturer has provided "as served" data using the method of cooking and/or other preparation that will be used in the school kitchen. In this case, the food item can be entered directly into the ingredient database).

The software will allow the user to enter the type of fat and percentages of moisture and fat losses directly into the recipe and make the calculations. Assume zero (0) moisture/fat change for food items that are only heated/reheated.

Refer to Appendix H to obtain common moisture losses and fat gains during deep-frying, and incorporate this information into the recipe.

KEY POINT

If a recipe for the fried product will need to be developed because there is no nutrient data available for moisture loss or fat gain, the database food/ingredient code for the commercially prepared food product, the database food/ingredient code for the type of fat used in frying, and the percentages of moisture loss and fat gain will have to be entered in the recipe.

Selecting the Correct Measure of a Food
Volume vs. Weight

When selecting data for the nutrient analysis, ensure the correct measure of food is selected. The unit of measure entered will depend on how the food is used in the recipe or menu. When selecting data, be sure the correct measure of food is entered, for example, teaspoon, gram, cup, gallon, pound or fluid ounce. If weight measures (oz, lb) are available for a recipe, it is more accurate to enter the weight measure.

When selecting the correct measure of a food, it is critical to know whether the food is measured by weight or by volume. **Any measure that is listed as ounce will be a weight measure, unless it is specifically designated as fluid ounces (fl. oz.) in the software.** Weight measures include grams, ounces, and pounds. Volume measures will be listed as teaspoons, tablespoons, fluid ounces, cups, pints, quarts, and gallons.

The chart below demonstrates nutrient analysis errors that can occur when volume measures are confused with weight measures.

Example: Selecting the Correct Measurement

Menu Items:
1/2 cup Raisin Bran
3/4 cup Canned Peaches
1 cup Spaghetti

	Weight (Incorrectly Entered)	Volume (Correctly Entered)
Raisin Bran	4 oz. = 356 calories	½ cup = 79 calories
Peaches	6 oz. = 92 calories	¾ cup = 102 calories
Spaghetti	8 oz. = 359	1 cup = 221 calories
NOTE: 4 oz. = ¼ pound (not ½ cup); 6 oz. = 3/8 pound (not ¾ cup); 8 oz. = ½ pound (not 1 cup) ½ cup = 4 fluid ounces; ¾ cup = 6 fluid ounces; 1 cup = 8 fluid ounces		

With all of these considerations in mind, the user can now begin to enter the data for a local recipe.

Steps to Entering a Local Recipe

You must follow your software directions as these directions may vary from software program to program.

STEP 1

Pre-Publication Copy

Enter recipe number

Most software programs will automatically assign a number as each new recipe is added.

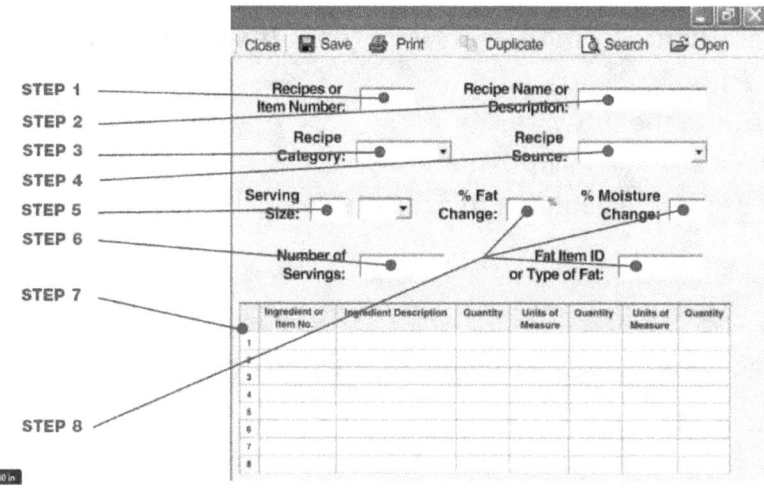

STEP 2
Enter the recipe name

For software that bases the "search" feature on the first word of the recipe name, it is important to develop a system that will help you locate your recipes. For example, a recipe for Baked Chicken could be listed as Chicken, Baked. This will allow you to find your recipe by searching "chicken". Refer to your software instructions for information about how to search in your software.

STEP 3
Identify the recipe category

For example, Entrees, Salads, Vegetables. This will also help if you need to search for a recipe.

STEP 4
Identify the source of the recipe

STEP 5
Enter the serving or portion size

For example, 1/2 cup, 2.25 oz. patty, 2" x 3" rectangle, 1 each.

Pre-Publication Copy

STEP 6
Enter the number of servings the recipe makes (yield)

STEP 7
Select the correct food items/ingredients from the software (or software program's database) and enter the correct amount
- View the food ingredients listed in the software.
- Select the correct food items or ingredients from the software.
- Enter the correct amount of each ingredient according to previous directions for the **Yield Factor Method.**

STEP 8
If applicable, enter the type of fat used for deep-frying and the percent moisture loss or fat gain for the recipe

Follow your software directions for entering this information. Refer to Appendix H for percent moisture loss or fat gains for selected products.

STEP 9
Compare the recipe entered in the software with your printed recipe to be sure that:

- the yield is correct,
- the serving size is correct,
- all ingredients are included,
- the correct food items were selected from the software's ingredient databases, and
- the amount of each ingredient is correct using the **Yield Factor Method.**

KEY POINT

Selecting the correct food item from the database is critical to accurate nutrient analysis. For example, if the SFA uses a firm hydrogenated soybean oil margarine but a soft corn oil margarine is selected from the CN Database, the nutrient analysis will be inaccurate.

STEP 10
Save the recipe

STEP 11
Check the recipe for data entry errors

Pre-Publication Copy

(See the section below on *How the Software Calculates Recipes*) This comparison can help to identify if there has been an error in the data entry of the recipe.

STEP 12
Print the recipe, including nutrient analysis

How the Software Calculates the Nutrient Analysis

When recipes are entered into the software, both a serving size and a recipe yield (the number of servings a recipe makes) are entered. It is important to know that the software calculates the nutrients in a serving based on the *number of servings in the recipe* (the yield), **not** based on the *size of the serving* entered. In addition, total nutrients in the recipe are divided by the number of servings to get the "per serving" analysis.

If the recipe has been entered accurately using the Yield Factor Method, the gram weight of one serving as calculated by the software should be close to the average actual gram weight of one serving.

> **(!)** **CAUTION:** Remember the software calculates a nutrient analysis by the yield (number of servings). When recipe ingredients or quantities are changed, the recipe yield is frequently changed. You must re-standardize the recipe, recalculate yield and enter a corrected yield, if applicable.

Checking Recipes for Error

The comparison of the gram weight of one serving as calculated by the computer with the actual average gram weight of one serving can be used to flag a recipe for possible errors. It is expected that there will be some variation in the two weights because nutrient analysis is not an exact science, and moisture loss may not always be accurately reflected in the calculations. A significant discrepancy between the two weights may indicate one of the following:

- an error in data entry, the recipe has not been standardized and either the yield or the serving size is inaccurate, or

- the Yield Factor Method has not been followed.

If the recipe is portioned using a scoop or measuring spoon, you probably do not know the weight of an average serving.

The following procedures can be used to calculate the weight of one serving of a recipe.

Pre-Publication Copy

- Prepare the recipe and carefully portion out 5 servings using the stated portion size. Using a gram scale, weigh each serving.

- Add the serving weights and divide the total by 5. This will give you an "average" serving weight.

- To get a better estimate of true serving weight, 2 persons should do the portioning and weighing of 5 samples each.

OR

Prepare the recipe, weigh the total quantity produced (minus weight of container) and divide by the number of servings (yield) of the recipe.

Creating a Recipe Variation
USDA Recipe Variations for Optional Ingredient(s)

When the school district/school is preparing a USDA recipe exactly as written with the only exception that they are simply adding an ingredient(s) that is listed as "optional" in the recipe (e.g., adding the optional ingredient, raisins, to Applesauce Cake), a new recipe should be created and named.

Example: Applesauce Cake with Raisins
           Source: Local

Because the nutrient profiles of all USDA Recipes are incorporated into the CN Database, the user would select the USDA recipe as a food item in the software's ingredient database and add it to the new recipe as a recipe ingredient. Then the user would need only to add the optional ingredient(s) to this new local recipe.

USDA Recipe Variation for Alternate Ingredient(s) or Other Modifications

When the SFA/school prepares a USDA recipe using an alternate ingredient(s) or make other changes to the recipe, you will need to create a new recipe using the Yield Factor Method by entering the ingredients and their amounts and saving it as a different recipe. Or, if the software company has entered the USDA recipes with its ingredients, you may copy the appropriate USDA recipe and review it carefully for accuracy. Then, following the Yield Factor Method, you may change the ingredient(s) and/or amount(s) as needed, and name and save it as a different recipe.

Modifying a Local Standardized Recipe

When adding a recipe variation such as alternate or optional ingredients to an existing recipe, you may modify the original recipe and then resave it. If you want to keep both recipe variations, you may copy the original recipe, make changes, rename, and save the recipe.

When local recipes are entered and saved to the recipe database in the software, you can:

- Change, add or delete food ingredients and amounts.
- Change preparation or serving instructions.

Single Serving Recipes

In addition, for nutrient analysis, recipes can be made for single servings, for example 1/2 cup French fries, 1 beef patty, 1 hotdog and bun. The software is required to calculate the ingredient amounts for a different number of servings for a recipe.

Creating a Theme Bar Recipe

Salad bars and other food bars, such as pasta bars, taco bars, deli bars, potato bars, and such can serve as the complete reimbursable lunch (except for milk) or as a food or menu item that is part of a reimbursable lunch depending on the food items on the bar and how it is structured. The recipe and nutrient analysis of the food bar is based on historical usage of food bar items.

Standardized recipes can be developed for food bars and entered into the software. The recipe should be constructed based on a "typical day".

To develop a standardized recipe for a theme bar:

Step 1: Determine the number of servings the recipe produces (yield). This would be the number of people who use the food bar, regardless of whether by students for reimbursable meals, by adults, or for a la carte sales.

Step 2: Determine the serving size. The serving size is the minimum quantity that the student must select to meet the meal pattern for the reimbursable meal. For example, for an entree salad, the minimum quantity might be 1 cup.

Step 3: Determine the amount of each ingredient in the recipe:

- Measure the amount of each ingredient placed on the food bar on a typical day (the amounts placed on the bar at the beginning of the meal service plus any additions to the bar during the meal service).

- Measure the amount of each ingredient left over on the food bar at the end of the meal service.

- Subtract the amount left over from the amount placed on the food bar for each ingredient to determine the amount of each ingredient to enter for the recipe.

After the recipe is entered into the database, it can be used in planning or analyzing a day's menu. The number of servings entered into the menu for nutrient analysis would be the estimated number of students who are expected to select a reimbursable meal from the food bar (or the estimated number of servings of the menu item which will be selected as part of a reimbursable meal, if the food bar does not offer a full meal).

A separate recipe must be developed for each variation of the food bar. For example, if you rotate two salad bars, one that features iceberg lettuce and another that features fresh spinach, two separate recipes need to be developed. If other ingredients vary, each separate combination would need a separate recipe.

Shortcut Hints for Data Entry for Menu Analysis: Creating Recipes to Simplify Data Entry

Most software allows you to create sub-menus of items served frequently together, such as milk or condiments/accompaniments and the sub-menus can be added to a menu.

In addition to your own standardized recipes that you will be entering in your software, there are "recipes" that you can create to make data entry speedier. These "recipes" are not actually recipes for food production but are data-entry shortcuts for analyzing menus. The use of shortcut data entry recipes will reduce the amount of data entry for each menu. These are menu item choices that do not vary from day to day and which have usage that has been documented to be consistent.

This shortcut is illustrated for milk:

- A school district's menus have consistent choices for milk, and consistent student selection from one meal to the next.

- Because weighted averaging is required, the milk shortcut data entry recipe must be based on the choices of milk available and the percentages consistently chosen.

Example for Weighted Averaging:
Three kinds of milk are offered every day: unflavored low-fat milk (1%), chocolate nonfat milk, and unflavored nonfat milk. Based on historical data, 25% of the milk offered (1/2 pint cartons) were unflavored low-fat milk (1%), 50% were chocolate nonfat milk, 25% were unflavored nonfat milk.

Pre-Publication Copy

The Data Entry Shortcut Milk Recipe was created as follows:

For 100 servings:
- 25 - 1/2 pints unflavored low-fat milk (1%),
- 50 - 1/2 pints chocolate nonfat milk
- 25 - 1/2 pints unflavored nonfat milk

KEY POINT

If a SFA/school uses a data entry shortcut recipe for milk, they must develop their own recipe using SFA/school data.

Other Shortcut Data Entry Recipes

Other shortcut data entry recipes for standardized choices can be created if the items offered do not vary and student choices are consistent (for districts using weighted averages). Some examples of menu items offered as standardized choices by SFAs/schools include fruit juices, cold cereals, and assorted salad dressings.

Creating shortcut data entry recipes for condiments/accompaniments is not recommended unless the exact condiments/accompaniments are offered each day, and students select the exact percentage of condiments/accompaniments (weighted averaging). Student selection and usage of condiments/accompaniments usually depends on the day's menu, so a condiment/accompaniment shortcut data entry recipe cannot be developed. For example, students may select catsup more frequently on days that hamburgers and French fries are offered.

Common Errors in Data Entry of Recipes

- Incorrect food item or ingredient selected

- Incorrect measurements, such as weight or volume errors, incorrect recipe serving sizes, etc.

- As Purchased weight used rather than Edible Portion (Yield Factor Method not used correctly)

- Recipes entered have not been standardized, or standardized recipes have been analyzed but not used in the SFA/schools.

Reminders:

- Carefully select the correct food item from the software's database.

- Choose the correct measurement, such as volume or weight.

- Use cooked weight for cooked foods. (May require conversion from the *Food Buying Guide*).

- Use only standardized recipes that are used in the SFA/schools. For example, a recipe for rolls must show the added nutrients, if butter or margarine is brushed on top of rolls.

Chapter 9:
Entering Menu Plans

CHAPTER OBJECTIVES

After reading this chapter, you will understand how to:
- Identify menu (site) names and associated Dietary Specifications for each age/grade group and menu type offered for breakfast and lunch.
- Determine the number of projected servings using weighted averages.
- Enter the portion size of each menu item.

The various nutrient analysis software programs may have a different order of steps necessary to establish menu plans for analysis, but the following steps should be common to all the software.

STEP 1: Identify Menu (Site) Name and Associated Age/Grade Nutrient Standards

Menu (Site) Names

Most software requires a separate data entry menu name or site name for each *age/grade group* used by the SFA. Menus are planned to meet the nutrient levels of each USDA established age/grade group and menu type offered for breakfast and lunch by adjusting the portion size of each menu item. It may not be necessary to re-enter menus for each age/grade group. All software allows the user to *copy* a menu and adjust portions or change menu items as needed.

Some software allows menus to be created and then allow the menu planner to assign them to schools (sites) and age/grade groups. Other software requires establishing the menu (site) name and age/grade group prior to entering menu data. Follow the procedures of your software.

KEY POINT

Menu Name and Site are terms used by various software programs; the terms may refer to an actual meal site or it may be used to refer to an age/grade group served at a site.

Pre-Publication Copy

Assigning Age/Grade Groups for Each Menu Type

Assign the USDA established age/grade groups and menu type offered to each specific menu name or site. These age/grade groups have dietary specifications preset in the software. Examples are:

- K – 5
- 6 – 8
- 9 – 12

The software has been programmed to adjust the dietary specifications to the age/grade grouping entered.

The SFA/State agency will establish menu names for the age/grade groups and menu types offered only for the school being reviewed.

Administrative Review

When the State agency conducts a nutrient analysis as part of an Administrative Review of an SFA, State staff will choose one week within the review period to evaluate the dietary specifications for breakfast and lunch at the selected school. The site is selected is based on results from the *Meal Compliance Risk Assessment Tool*. The State agency will collect the menu documentation for each USDA established age/grade group and menu types offered at breakfast and lunch, and conduct a weighted nutrient analysis of all menu and food items (including condiments) offered as part of the reimbursable meal. In other words, a separate nutrient analysis is required for each age/grade group at the selected review site and if the review site has different menu offerings for different segments of students in the school, separate analyses are required for each population segment.

Example:

A school serving 6-12 graders plans two different lunch menus, one menu for 6-8 and another menu for 9-12. In this case, the school is offering two different lunch menus for different segments of students in the school. The SA will need to conduct two weighted nutrient analyses for lunch: one for the 6-8th grade students and one for 9-12th grade students to ensure each menu type meets the dietary specifications.

The school selected for review is representative of how the SFA is implementing the meal pattern. The State agency will assess compliance by comparing the nutrient analysis results to the Dietary Specifications requirements for the age/grade groups served in the school.

STEP 2: Identify Menu or Meal Types

The type of meal offered must be entered because there are specific program requirements for each meal:
- Lunch
- Breakfast

NOTE: State agencies may not combine breakfast and lunch nutrient analyses. Separate analyses make it easier to identify problems and target technical assistance.

STEP 3: Enter Individual Menus

Entering Individual Menus
The initial process in developing menus is to identify the menu items or recipes to be included for each menu. The software allows the user to search for the recipes or menu items either by identification code or by name of food or recipe. The identification code is the number assigned to each food or recipe. The software will also allow the menu planner to enter the name of the food or recipe, and it will **search** for the foods or recipe.

In the example below, the menu planner enters "Beef Stew" as the menu item and searches the database for the Beef Stew recipe.

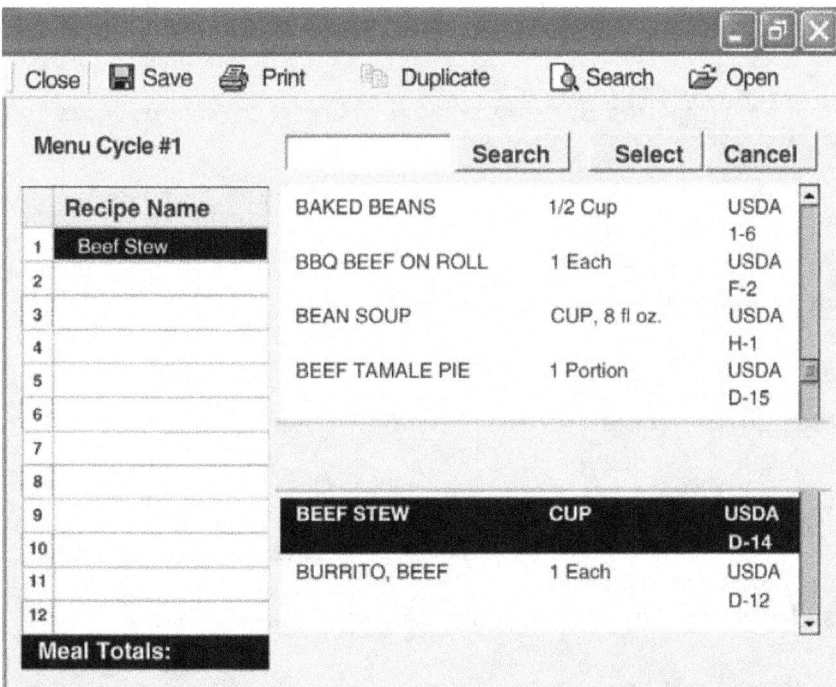

Cycle Menus

A cycle menu is a series of individual menus that are repeated on a periodic basis; they can save the user time in menu planning, data entry, and analysis. Most software allows the user to develop and enter cycle menus by means of a series of pre-numbered menus, and then allows the user to select and copy these menus to either calendars or cycles. SFAs may vary in the way they implement cycle menus.

KEY POINT

State agencies setting up menus for nutrient analysis during an Administrative Review will only enter menus for the designated school for the review week.

Some SFAs may repeat the same set of menus every four weeks or so, but have different sets of cycle menus for fall, winter, and spring. Some SFAs, especially those that do a lot of on-site preparation, may establish a basic number of menus and then vary or switch the scheduling of the individual menus depending on the day of the week and the amount of pre-preparation required.

STEP 4: Assign Dates to Menus and Determine Date Range for Nutrient Analysis

Software allows the user to select and copy menus to either calendars or cycles. The user determines the date range for analysis. A week for nutrient analysis purposes is 3-7 consecutive school days. If there are fewer than three consecutive days in a week, the days in that week are combined with the subsequent or previous week for analysis.

STEP 5: Determine Number of Servings and Serving Sizes (Portions) of Menu Items

Only menu/food items offered as part of reimbursable meals are analyzed. To conduct a weighted analysis, the user must project the number of servings for each menu item based on weighted averages (i.e., give more weight to menu items that students select more often).

KEY POINT

Weighted averages must be used for nutrient analyses. This means that all menu items must be weighted, including milk types and condiments/accompaniments.

If the State agency conducts the nutrient analysis for the Administrative Review, it will select one school using the Meal Compliance Risk Assessment Tool, request the menu documentation from the school for the week selected for review, and use the actual number of offered servings used in reimbursable meals to conduct a weighted analysis.

A More Detailed Explanation of Weighted Averaging
In the following example of weighted averaging, there are three entree choices in the meal. On average, 200 students normally receive a reimbursable meal for this age/grade grouping in the

school. A review of past production records of this meal indicates that pizza is more frequently selected and should be weighted accordingly.

Sample Weighted Averaging Of Three Entrée Choices

Weighted Nutrient Analysis of Entrees			
Entrée Items	Actual Servings Planned	Data Entry Servings Planned	Contribution to Nutrition Analysis
Pizza	100	100	50%
Baked Chicken	50	50	25%
Chef's Salad	50	50	25%
Total	200	200	100%

For weighted averaging, the total number of offered reimbursable meals with numbers of servings for each menu item, excluding food items sold as adult meals and a la carte, is required for each menu.

To conduct weighted nutrient analysis, the reviewer must enter the following items:

- Total number of offered reimbursable meals for each day of the weekly menu by age/grade grouping (Example: K - 5, 6 – 8, 9 -12);

- Portion size(s) for each menu item and condiment/accompaniment for each age/grade grouping; and

- Projected number of servings for each portion size of each menu item that will be part of the day's reimbursable meal, including milk and condiments/accompaniments and excluding a la carte and adult servings.

STEP 6: Create Applicable Reports for Review

- Day by Day Analysis
- Weekly Analysis

The software allows the user to create various reports as needed to check data entry. These include a menu spreadsheet indicating weekly analysis. These reports can be reviewed to identify missing data and/or errors in data entry.

Common Errors in Data Entry of Menus
- Incorrect food item/recipe selected from database

- Portion or serving sizes wrong

- Numbers for weighted averaging are incorrect

- Condiments/accompaniments are not entered as menu items, e.g., mayonnaise, mustard and/or catsup for hamburgers

- Menu item left off of the nutrient analysis, e.g., bun for hamburger

Reminders:

- Carefully select the correct food item/recipe from the database. Make sure that all recipes reflect the currently purchased food items.

- Choose the correct portion size.

- Make sure the numbers for production for weighted averaging have been done correctly.

- Review data entry to check for all menu items and condiments/accompaniments before saving menu.

Chapter 10:
Evaluating and Modifying Menus and Recipes to Meet the Dietary Specifications

> **CHAPTER OBJECTIVES**
>
> **After reading this chapter, you will understand how to:**
> - Evaluate how well current menus meet the Dietary Specifications.
> - Evaluate the menus for variety.
> - Modify the menus to meet the Dietary Specifications.
> - Include substitutions in the analysis.
> - Decide when to adjust future menus.

Evaluate menus

The final process of nutrient analysis is to evaluate the menus and modify accordingly to meet the Dietary Specifications.

Review daily and weekly nutrient analyses.

1. Evaluate the nutrient analysis of menus

Evaluate how well the current menu meets the Dietary Specifications. This will help to determine what, if any, changes must be made.

- How do the menus compare to the Dietary Specifications? What areas need changes? Which areas are okay?
- Do the menus have calories within an allowable range? Remember the importance of consistent calorie levels.
- Are the menus too high in saturated fat or sodium?

2. Review menus for variety by looking at the frequency with which menu items are offered

The **frequency** with which a particular food or type of food is offered will affect the nutrient content of the menu.

- Are a variety of meats/meat alternates, fruits, vegetables, and grains offered?
- Are sufficient quantities of vegetables from all the subgroups offered?
- What proportions of grains offered are whole grain-rich?

- Should the total number of low fat or low unsaturated fat food or menu items be increased?
- Are too many high sodium items offered?
- Can a popular high fat or high sodium item be offered fewer times in a cycle or week?

3. Review Portion Sizes

After making adjustments to how often foods are offered, recheck the nutrient analysis. If there are still discrepancies, look at the **portion size** of problem foods next.

- Can a smaller serving be offered of popular foods that may be contributing too many calories, or too much saturated fat or sodium?
- Can the quantity of a high fat ingredient in a recipe be reduced?
- Can a high fat ingredient in a recipe be changed to a lower fat ingredient?
- Can the portion size of a menu item be increased to meet minimum calorie levels?

4. Check for "Balance"

Next, look at the **balance** of foods within each day and the week.

- Are the colors in the menu pleasing to the eye?
- Are the food flavor combinations pleasing to the taste?
- Does the menu have pleasing contrasts in shapes and sizes, textures, and temperatures?
- Are there too many foods high in saturated fat or sodium in the same day or the same week?
- Can a high fat or sodium entree be balanced with low fat or reduced sodium side dishes or other low fat or reduced sodium entrees during the week?

Using the Nutrient Food Source List

If the Dietary Specifications have still not been met, search the **Nutrient Food Source List** in the software to find ideas for menu modification.

This list suggests foods that might be added or substituted in menus in order to increase the amount of a particular nutrient found to be below the nutrient standard in the week's breakfasts or lunches.

When replacing a food, be sure that the levels of the other nutrients in the menu are maintained. After deciding which foods to change or which foods to add to the menu, the menu must be edited, nutrient values need to be recalculated and compared to the Dietary Specifications.

Re-create Appropriate Reports for Re-analysis

Pre-Publication Copy

After modifications have been made, create the appropriate reports to review the new nutrient analyses. If nutrient targets have still not been met, continue the process described above until the Dietary Specifications have been met.

Substitutions

Occasionally it may be necessary to make a substitution to a planned menu due to various reasons such as food shortage, improper delivery from vendors, or effective use of leftovers. This is a concern because:

- Substitutions *change* the nutrient content; and

- Meals *may or may not* continue to meet the Dietary Specifications.

If a substitution is made to the offered menu, the substitution must be included in the nutrient analysis.

SFAs are expected to make substitutions only due to unforeseen circumstances. Remember, reimbursable meals are based on the ability to meet the Dietary Specifications. Some examples include:

- Food shortage (food not delivered);

- Improper delivery (incorrect product delivered),

- Crop failure (food unavailable);

- Significant cost increase in food items; and

- Effective use of leftovers (see *Leftovers* below).

USDA strongly encourages "like" substitutions, such as spinach for romaine lettuce, but meals are compliant if the daily and weekly requirements are met.

Leftovers

If leftovers are offered to students on the serving line as part of the reimbursable meal, they must be included in weighted nutrient analyses and are subject to the weekly Dietary Specifications. Leftovers offered to students during the same meal in which are initially offered are considered seconds.

Foods offered as leftovers must be entered into the nutrient analysis *once*. For example, 100 servings of carrots are offered on Monday, and 20 servings are leftover. The 20 leftover carrot servings are offered Tuesday. The nutrient analysis should be conducted on the menu as offered: Monday's offerings should reflect 100 servings of carrots, even though 20 leftover servings were offered on Tuesday. The Dietary Specifications requirements are weekly requirements, and the nutrient analysis would still reflect that 100 servings of carrots were offered over the week, even if some leftovers were offered on subsequent days. It is important NOT to enter 100 servings of carrots Monday, and 20 servings of carrots Tuesday because this would result in double counting carrots.

In an effort to reduce waste, a SFA may serve leftovers in a subsequent meal period. This could include serving breakfast leftovers at lunch, or serving lunch leftovers at breakfast. Menu planners should not plan to have leftovers, so this is expected to be a rare occurrence. If leftovers are being carried from breakfast to lunch (or vice versa), there is no need to reanalyze these leftovers.

SFAs may also freeze leftovers and serve them first on the serving line, following standard HACCP protocols, the next time that particular item reappears in the menu cycle. Schools are cautioned that any leftover not frozen for reuse should be used within a safe period. Bacteria continue to grow even under refrigeration.

The State has discretion to determine whether the amount and frequency of leftovers are reasonable. **If the school consistently has leftovers to add to each day's menus, schools need to consider participation trends in an effort to provide one reimbursable lunch for each child every day.**

Documentation

Documentation of substitutions and leftover usage, and the date the need for a substitution or leftover usage was known, must be maintained by making notes on the menu production records.

Adjusting Future Menus

The menus have now been planned, offered, served, and analyzed. Before the menu is used again, the actual participation and the actual number of menu items offered (recorded on the production record) should be compared to the numbers planned. If the differences are such that production numbers need to be adjusted, then the menu should be reanalyzed using the new numbers.

Additionally, menus need re-analyzing whenever:

Pre-Publication Copy

- Menu/food items change;

- Food products change, including commercially prepared products;

- Recipes change; or

- There is any change that will affect the nutrient content of the meals, such as a change in foods selected, which changes the weighting.

Getting Help

Any questions that may arise about food items, recipe analysis, or menu analysis that have not been addressed in this manual should be communicated to your FNS Regional Office.

Appendix A:

Meal Pattern for Required Grade Groups: Breakfast and Lunch

	Breakfast Meal Pattern			Lunch Meal Pattern		
	Grades K-5[a]	Grades 6-8[a]	Grades 9-12[a]	Grades K-5	Grades 6-8	Grades 9-12
Meal Pattern	Amount of Food[b] Per Week (Minimum Per Day)					
Fruits (cups)[c,d]	5 (1)[e]	5 (1)[e]	5 (1)[e]	2½ (½)	2½ (½)	5 (1)
Vegetables (cups)[c,d]	0	0	0	3¾ (¾)	3¾ (¾)	5 (1)
Dark green[f]	0	0	0	½	½	½
Red/Orange[f]	0	0	0	¾	¾	1¼
Beans/Peas (Legumes)[f]	0	0	0	½	½	½
Starchy[f]	0	0	0	½	½	½
Other[f,g]	0	0	0	½	½	¾
Additional Veg to Reach Total[h]	0	0	0	1	1	1½
Grains (oz eq)[i]	7-10 (1)[j]	8-10 (1)[j]	9-10 (1)[j]	8-9 (1)	8-10 (1)	10-12 (2)
Meats/Meat Alternates (oz eq)	0[k]	0[k]	0[k]	8-10 (1)	9-10 (1)	10-12 (2)
Fluid milk (cups)[l]	5 (1)	5 (1)	5 (1)	5 (1)	5 (1)	5 (1)
Other Specifications: Daily Amount Based on the Average for a 5-Day Week						
Min-max cals (kcal)[m,n,o]	350-500	400-550	450-600	550-650	600-700	750-850
Saturated fat (% of total calories)[n,o]	< 10	< 10	< 10	< 10	< 10	< 10
Sodium (mg)[n,p]	≤ 430	≤ 470	≤ 500	≤ 640	≤ 710	≤ 740
Trans fat[n,o]	Nutrition label or manufacturer specifications must indicate zero grams of underline trans fat per serving.					

[a] In the SBP, the above age-grade groups are required beginning July 1, 2013 (SY 2013-14). In SY 2012-2013 only, schools may continue to use the meal pattern for grades K-12 (see § 220.23).

^b Food items included in each food group and subgroup and amount equivalents. Minimum creditable serving is ⅛ cup.

^c One quarter-cup of dried fruit counts as ½ cup of fruit; 1 cup of leafy greens counts as ½ cup of vegetables. No more than half of the fruit or vegetable offerings may be in the form of juice. All juice must be 100% full-strength.

^d For breakfast, vegetables may be substituted for fruits, but the first two cups per week of any such substitution must be from the dark green, red/orange, beans and peas (legumes) or "Other vegetables" subgroups as defined in §210.10(c)(2)(iii).

^e The fruit quantity requirement for the SBP (5 cups/week and a minimum of 1 cup/day) is effective July 1, 2014 (SY 2014-2015).

^f Larger amounts of these vegetables may be served.

^g This category consists of "Other vegetables" as defined in §210.10(c)(2)(iii)(E). For the purposes of the NSLP, "Other vegetables" requirement may be met with any additional amounts from the dark green, red/orange, and beans/peas (legumes) vegetable subgroups as defined in §210.10(c)(2)(iii).

^h Any vegetable subgroup may be offered to meet the total weekly vegetable requirement.

ⁱ At least half of the grains offered must be whole grain-rich in the NSLP beginning July 1, 2012 (SY 2012-2013), and in the SBP beginning July 1, 2013 (SY 2013-2014). All grains must be whole grain-rich in both the NSLP and the SBP beginning July 1, 2014 (SY 2014-15).

^j In the SBP, the grain ranges must be offered beginning July 1, 2013 (SY 2013-2014).

^k There is no separate meat/meat alternate component in the SBP. Beginning July 1, 2013 (SY 2013-2014), schools may substitute 1 oz. eq. of meat/meat alternate for 1 oz. eq. of grains after the minimum daily grains requirement is met.

^l Fluid milk must be low-fat (1 percent milk fat or less, unflavored) or fat-free (unflavored or flavored).

^m The average daily amount of calories for a 5-day school week must be within the range (at least the minimum and no more than the maximum values).

ⁿ Discretionary sources of calories (solid fats and added sugars) may be added to the meal pattern if within the specifications for calories, saturated fat, trans fat, and sodium. Foods of minimal nutritional value and fluid milk with fat content greater than 1 percent milk fat are not allowed.

^o In the SBP, calories and trans fat specifications take effect beginning July 1, 2013 (SY 2013-2014).

^p Final sodium specifications are to be reached by SY 2022-2023 or July 1, 2022. Intermediate sodium specifications are established for SY 2014-2015 and 2017-2018. See required intermediate specifications in § 210.10(f)(3) for lunches and § 220.8(f)(3) for breakfasts.

Age/Grade Group	Baseline: Current Average Sodium Levels As Offered[1] (mg)	Sodium Reduction: Timeline & Amount			% Change (Current Levels vs. Final Targets)
		Target 1: Meet by July 1, 2014 (SY 2014-2015) (mg)	Target 2: Meet by July 1, 2017 (SY 2017-2018) (mg)	Final Target:[2] Meet by July 1, 2022 (SY 2022-2023) (mg)	
School Breakfast Program					
K-5	573 (elementary)	$\leq$ 540 (28.4% of UL)	$\leq$ 485 (25.5% of UL)	$\leq$ 430 (22.6% of UL)	-25%
6-8	629 (middle)	$\leq$ 600 (27.3% of UL)	$\leq$ 535 (24.3% of UL)	$\leq$ 470 (21.4% of UL)	-25%
9-12	686 (high)	$\leq$ 640 (27.8% of UL)	$\leq$ 570 (24.8% of UL)	$\leq$ 500 (21.7% of UL)	-27%
National School Lunch Program					
K-5	1,377 (elementary)	$\leq$ 1,230 (64.8% of UL)	$\leq$ 935 (49.2% of UL)	$\leq$ 640 (33.7% of UL)	-54%
6-8	1,520 (middle)	$\leq$ 1,360 (61.8% of UL)	$\leq$ 1,035 (47.0% of UL)	$\leq$ 710 (32.3% of UL)	-53%
9-12	1,588 (high)	$\leq$ 1,420 (61.7% of UL)	$\leq$ 1,080 (47.0% of UL)	$\leq$ 740 (32.2% of UL)	-53%

[1]Current Average Sodium Levels as Offered are from the School Nutrition and Dietary Assessment Study-III. Data were collected in the 2004-05 school year.

[2]The IOM final targets are based on the Tolerable Upper Intake Limits (ULs) for sodium, established in the Dietary Reference Intakes (DRI) (IOM, 2004). The sodium ULs for school-aged children are 2,300 mg (ages 14-18), 2,200 mg (ages 9-13), and 1,900 mg (ages 4-8). The final sodium targets represent the UL for each age/grade group multiplied by the percentage of nutrients supplied by each meal (approximately 21.5% for breakfast, 32% for lunch), as recommended by IOM. IOM's recommended final sodium targets for the K-5 age/grade group breakfasts and lunches are slightly higher than 21.5% and 32% 32%, respectively, of the UL because this proposed elementary school group spans part of two DRI age groups (ages 4–8 and 9–13 years).

Appendix B: Nutrient Analysis and Validation Checklist

General Information	
SFA/School:	
Agreement Number:	
Contact/Title:	
Phone:	
Email:	
Address:	
Reviewer(s):	
Nutrient Analysis conducted by:	
Date of on-site review:	

Complete the on-site portion of the Dietary Specifications Assessment Tool to gather useful information to conduct/validate the nutrient analysis.

Comments – Areas of Concern – Follow Up Items

Other CN Programs	Age/Grades	General Information
Breakfast ☐ Snack ☐	Ages/Grades in School: Ages/Grades for Menu Planning: Lunch: K-5 ☐ 6-8 ☐ 9-12 ☐ Breakfast: K-5 ☐ 6-8 ☐ 9-12 ☐	Check Box if Yes: Offer vs Serve ☐ A la carte sales available ☐ Adult Meals ☐ Special Needs Meals ☐

DAY OF REVIEW MENU		
LUNCH MENU	**PLANNED SERVING SIZE**	**ACTUAL SERVING SIZE**
LUNCH CONDIMENTS	**PLANNED SERVING SIZE**	**ACTUAL SERVING SIZE**

Pre-Publication Copy

BREAKFAST MENU – (if applicable)	PLANNED SERVING SIZE	ACTUAL SERVING SIZE
BREAKFAST CONDIMENTS	PLANNED SERVING SIZE	ACTUAL SERVING SIZE

	YES	NO	COMMENTS
1) The on-site portion of the DIETARY SPECIFICATIONS ASSESSMENT TOOL is complete • On-site observation using Dietary Specifications Assessment Tool was conducted to ensure an accurate nutrient analysis is performed or validated.	☐	☐	
2) Is the targeted menu review site in compliance with the meal pattern requirements (meal components and quantities)?	☐	☐	
3) If required, has the SFA/school implemented corrective action as agreed to during the on-site review to ensure the appropriate source documents are accurate before starting the nutrient analysis process? • If YES, proceed with conducting a nutrient analysis. • If NO, immediate corrective action is required. Establish a time frame for the school to locate or develop the necessary documentation for the reviewer to perform an accurate nutrient analysis. Conduct analysis once documentation is received. • If documentation is not received by the established date, proceed with noncompliance actions (i.e., withholding funds).	☐	☐	N/A ☐
Source Documents Required For Analysis/Validation	**YES**	**NO**	**COMMENTS**
Review all documentation the SFA provided in support of menus for the menu/nutrient analysis evaluation. Indicate whether the school/SFA provided the following documentation/materials needed to complete/validate the nutrient analysis. Request additional information, if needed.			

	YES	NO	COMMENTS
Are the necessary materials available?	☐	☐	
a. Menus	☐	☐	
• The reviewer should conduct a weighted nutrient analysis based on meals offered for each USDA established age/grade group and menu type offered at lunch and breakfast.			
b. Production records include all required information for each age/grade group and menu type	☐	☐	
• Production records (including salad bar/theme bar production records) must list all food or menu items offered as part of the reimbursable meal. Additional items such as condiments, gelatin, butter, must also be included. Portion sizes, total food quantity used to prepare each menu item or food item, and leftovers must be recorded.			
c. Number of a la carte sales, adult, and "other" meals differentiated on production records	☐	☐	
• If the same food items are used for reimbursable meals, a la carte sales and/or "other" meals (e.g., adult meals, meals for special diets), production records differentiate the number of menu items planned for each type of meal, or for a la carte sales.			
d. Standardized recipes include preparation instructions, portion sizes and yield used in the menus for the period of evaluation.	☐	☐	
e. Nutrition information is available for commercially prepared foods (e.g., Nutrition Facts Labels or Manufacturer's Data Submission Forms).	☐	☐	
f. Food product descriptions/specifications indicate the specific form of the foods used (e.g., canned in light syrup, frozen, no added salt, 1 % low fat milk).	☐	☐	
g. Crediting Information is available.	☐	☐	
• CN labels are useful because they give information on creditable food items for identifying a food-based reimbursable meal and help to identify specific commercially prepared foods in the CN Database. However, Child Nutrition labels do not provide nutrient information for data input when conducting a nutrient analysis.			

	YES	NO	COMMENTS
PROCEED BELOW ONLY IF VALIDATING AN EXISTING NUTRIENT ANALYSIS			
VALIDATING NUTRIENT ANALYSIS CHECKLIST	**YES**	**NO**	**COMMENTS**

1) Was the nutrient analysis software:
  a) USDA approved?
    • If SFA is not using USDA-approved software to conduct their nutrient analysis, the SA must conduct a nutrient analysis.
	☐	☐	

b) Using most recent version of CN database? • It is important for schools to update their software in order to ensure they are using the updated CN Database, as it will ensure a more accurate nutrient analysis. Software companies may issue newer versions of their software to update computer functions that are not related to the CN Database. The version of the software and CN Database release is generally located under the "Help" pull-down menu. If not, the SFA may need to contact the software company to determine the version they are currently using.	☐	☐	
2) What credentials, qualifications, and/or training, does menu planner have? • Record the qualifications of the computer specialist who will enter data. List any credentials, training, and/or related experience.	☐	☐	
3) Are source documents missing that prevent the reviewer from validating the analysis?	☐	☐	
4) Were the appropriate Age/Grade groups used? • Determine if the age/grade groups used are appropriate. Review the nutrient analysis printout to determine if the age/grade groups entered are appropriate to the age/grade groups used for menu planning and portioning.	☐	☐	

5) Was a separate analysis completed for breakfast and lunch, each age/grade group, and each menu type?
  • Determine if separate analyses were completed for breakfast and lunch.
  • A separate nutrient analysis is required for each age/grade group. Also, if a school has different menu offerings for different segments of students in the school, separate analyses are required for each population segment.
	☐	☐	

Pre-Publication Copy

	YES	NO	COMMENTS
6) Validating weighted averaging: Interview the menu planner to determine the method used to calculate the number of offered menu items. Does the method described yield a correct weighted nutrient analysis?	☐	☐	
• If the answer is "No", reviewer must provide the necessary TA and request immediate corrective action. • If the answer is "Yes" meaning that the method used seems reasonable, validate the weighted nutrient analysis:			
a. Was the weighting done correctly?	☐	☐	
○ If the weighted averaging was done for the individual school, determine if it was done correctly. Was the weighting of individual menu or food items based on information from past production records at the school?			
b. Were a la carte sales, adult meals, and special needs meals excluded from the analysis?	☐	☐	
7) Were all menu and food items, condiments, and foods of minimal nutritional value served as part of a menu item, included in the nutrient analysis?	☐	☐	
• Determine if the school included all offered menu and food items, condiments, and foods of minimal nutritional value (served as part of a menu item) in the nutrient analysis. • Condiments or any other food item located after the point of service must be included in the analysis if they are part of a menu item or associated with a reimbursable meal. For example, if a packet of catsup (9 grams) is made available for hamburgers, the menu should include the projected number of packets historically served. If condiments are available in bulk, the total amount usually used for a meal should be recorded.			
8) Were recipes entered using the "yield factor method"?	☐	☐	
• Determine if recipes and ingredients were entered into the database using the Yield Factor Method." • Refer to guidance manual *Nutrient Analysis Protocols for the School Meals Nutrition Program: How to Analyze Menus for USDA's School Meal Programs* for information on using the yield factor method. • The Yield Factor Method requires that each raw ingredient in a recipe be converted and entered into the			

	YES	NO	COMMENTS
recipe database as ready-to-serve or cooked.			
9) Did the SFA/school reanalyze menus based on changes in student selections and participation? • Review the production records for a minimum of one day during the review week and compare to a day(s) in a previous menu cycle. Determine if the school/SFA is adjusting the number of menu items offered according to student preference.	☐	☐	
10) Are menus being reanalyzed based on changes in purchased products? • Review a sample of purchased products to verify that changes are made to the ingredient and/or recipe database when new products are purchased.	☐	☐	

11) Did the SFA/school input nutrient data correctly for:
    a. Local or USDA modified recipes?
    b. Food items not in the database?
 	
• Through interview and/or review of the local database, determine if the school/SFA input nutrient data correctly.
• Obtain a sample of the standardized recipes that the school/SFA entered into the database and determine that each recipe has been accurately entered into the database, using the "Yield Factor Method."
• Compare the data entered to the nutrition facts label for the product or information submitted by the product manufacturer.
• Evaluate the detailed summary for % values that appear too high or too low for specific menu items or nutrient averages. This is an indication that either the ingredient or the recipe was entered incorrectly.
    o If data were not entered correctly, determine if the problem is systemic or non-systemic.
    o Ingredients and recipes need to be entered accurately in order to generate a reliable nutrient analysis. Frequent data entry errors (e.g., recipes that are missing ingredients, incorrect yields, incorrect nutrients entered for products, incorrect portion size assigned to nutrients) indicate a systemic problem.
	☐
	☐
		☐
		☐	

12) Can the reviewer validate the accuracy of the nutrient analysis? • Determine if the reviewer can validate that the	☐	☐	

	YES	NO	COMMENTS
nutrient analysis was conducted accurately and correctly and reflects the SFA's planned menu(s). • If NO, provide TA and request immediate corrective action. If SFA is unable to implement corrective action, the SA must conduct the nutrient analysis.	☐	☐	

Appendix C: Foods of Minimal Nutritional Value*

The following is taken from Appendix B of 7 CFR Part 210.

Appendix B to Part 210--Categories of Foods of Minimal Nutritional Value

(a) Foods of minimal nutritional value--Foods of minimal nutritional value are:

(1) Soda Water--A class of beverages made by absorbing carbon dioxide in potable water. The amount of carbon dioxide used is not less than that which will be absorbed by the beverage at a pressure of one atmosphere and at a temperature of 60 deg. F. It either contains no alcohol or only such alcohol, not in excess of 0.5 percent by weight of the finished beverage, as is contributed by the flavoring ingredient used. No product shall be excluded from this definition because it contains artificial sweeteners or discrete nutrients added to the food such as vitamins, minerals and protein.

(2) Water Ices--As defined by 21 CFR 135.160 Food and Drug Administration Regulations except that water ices which contain fruit or fruit juices are not included in this definition.

(3) Chewing Gum--Flavored products from natural or synthetic gums and other ingredients which form an insoluble mass for chewing.

(4) Certain Candies--Processed foods made predominantly from sweeteners or artificial sweeteners with a variety of minor ingredients which characterize the following types:

(i) Hard Candy--A product made predominantly from sugar (sucrose) and corn syrup which may be flavored and colored, is characterized by a hard, brittle texture, and includes such items as sour balls, fruit balls, candy sticks, lollipops, starlight mints, after dinner mints, sugar wafers, rock candy, cinnamon candies, breath mints, jaw breakers and cough drops.

(ii) Jellies and Gums--A mixture of carbohydrates which are combined to form a stable gelatinous system of jelly-like character, and are generally flavored and colored, and include gum drops, jelly beans, jellied and fruit-flavored slices.

(iii) Marshmallow Candies--An aerated confection composed as sugar, corn syrup, invert sugar, 20 percent water and gelatin or egg white to which flavors and colors may be added.

(iv) Fondant--A product consisting of microscopic-sized sugar crystals which are separated by thin film of sugar and/or invert sugar in solution such as candy corn, soft mints.

(v) Licorice--A product made predominantly from sugar and corn syrup which is flavored with an extract made from the licorice root.

(vi) Spun Candy--A product that is made from sugar that has been boiled at high temperature and spun at a high speed in a special machine.

(vii) Candy Coated Popcorn--Popcorn which is coated with a mixture made predominantly from sugar and corn syrup.

(b) Petitioning Procedures--Reconsideration of the list of foods of minimal nutritional value identified in paragraph (a) of this section may be pursued as follows:

(1) Any person may submit a petition to FNS requesting that an individual food be exempted from a category of foods of minimal nutritional value listed in paragraph (a). In the case of artificially sweetened foods, the petition must include a statement of the percent of Reference Daily Intake (RDI) for the eight nutrients listed in Sec. 210.11(a)(2) ``Foods of minimal nutritional value,'' that the food provides per serving and the petitioner's source of this information. In the case of all other foods, the petition must include a statement of the percent of RDI for the eight nutrients listed in Sec. 210.11(a)(2) ``Foods of minimal nutritional value,'' that the food provides per serving and per 100 calories and the petitioner's source of this information. The Department will determine whether or not the individual food is a food of minimal nutritional value as defined in Sec. 210.11(a)(2) and will inform the petitioner in writing of such determination, and the public by notice in the Federal Register as indicated below under paragraph (b)(3) of this section. In determining whether an individual food is a food of minimal nutritional value, discrete nutrients added to the food will not be taken into account.

(2) Any person may submit a petition to FNS requesting that foods in a particular category of foods be classified as foods of minimal nutritional value as defined in Sec. 210.11(a)(2). The petition must identify and define the food category in easily understood language, list examples of the food contained in the category and include a list of ingredients which the foods in that category usually contain. If, upon review of the petition, the Department determines that the foods in that category should not be classified as foods of minimal nutritional value, the petitioners will be so notified in writing. If, upon review of the petition, the Department determines that there is a substantial likelihood that the foods in that category should be classified as foods of minimal nutritional value as defined in Sec. 210.11(a)(2), the Department shall at that time inform the petitioner. In addition, the Department shall publish a proposed rule restricting the sale of foods in that category, setting forth the reasons for this action, and soliciting public comments. On the basis of comments received within 60 days of publication of the proposed rule and other available information, the Department will determine whether the nutrient composition of the foods indicates that the category should be classified as a category of foods of minimal nutritional value. The petitioner shall be notified in writing and the public shall be notified of the Department's final determination upon publication in the Federal Register as indicated under paragraph (b)(3) of this section.

(3) By May 1 and November 1 of each year, the Department will amend appendix B to exclude those individual foods identified under paragraph (b)(1) of this section, and to include those

categories of foods identified under paragraph (b)(2) of this section, provided, that there are necessary changes. The schedule for amending appendix B is as follows:

	Publication	
Actions for publication	May	November
Deadline for receipt of petitions by USDA.	Nov. 15	May 15
USDA to notify petitioners of results of Departmental review and publish proposed rule (if applicable).	Feb. 1	Aug. 1
60 Day comment period	Feb. 1 through Apr. 1	Aug. 1 through Oct. 1
Public notice of amendment of appendix B by	May 1	Nov. 1

(4) Written petitions should be sent to the Chief, Technical Assistance Branch, Nutrition and Technical Services Division, FNS, USDA, Alexandria, Virginia 22302, on or before November 15 or May 15 of each year. Petitions must include all information specified in paragraph (b) of this appendix and Sec. 220.12(b) (1) or (2) as appropriate.

*NOTE: This appendix applies to SY 2013-14 only. It will be removed for SY 2014-15, when the Smart Snacks standards are implemented.

Appendix D: USDA-Approved Nutrient Analysis Software Requirements

Description of Software Requirements and Functions

• Nutrient Standard Menu Planning software, which meets the specifications for use in the Child Nutrition Program, must comply with the following criteria:

• All of the appropriate files and fields from the Child Nutrition (CN) Database must be incorporated into the software (standard reference foods, USDA standardized recipe food items, commodity foods, manufacturer's foods, weights and measures, and the USDA *Food Buying Guide*).

• Users cannot alter information provided by the CN Database; however, user-entered information can be edited or deleted.

• The user will be able to enter new food items into a local database from information provided in a manufacturer's fact sheet or food label in nutrients per serving or specific weight, or percent of the Daily Reference Value (DRV).

• The software will automatically convert measures for weight and volume (if available) at all levels of item entry, recipe development, and menu planning.

• The user will be able to enter recipes; the software will produce a recipe report that includes the recipe code number, recipe name, serving/portion size, yield of the recipe based on number of servings, ingredients, the amount of each ingredient in units appropriate for food service, preparation instructions, and nutrient value of the recipe per serving or per 100 g (with nutrient changes calculated due to moisture/fat factors).

• The Recipe Nutrient Composition Report will contain the nutrient value contributed by each ingredient and the total nutrient value of the recipe per serving or per 100 g. The yield of the recipe will be able to be accurately adjusted to meet the needs of the food service without degrading the base recipe.

• A Recipe/Ingredient Cross Reference report will identify recipes that contain a certain food ingredient.

• Menus for a specific site can be developed and copied to another site or data range and the serving sizes adjusted for various age groups.

• Menu Reports will be available in both calendar and report formats.

• A Menu Production Record can be printed for use by foodservice workers to determine the

Pre-Publication Copy

quantities and serving sizes of food to prepare for a specific site. The Standard and Modified RDA data sets provided USDA are incorporated into the software and used for comparison in nutrient analyses.

• A Weighted Nutrient Analysis of an individual menu or range of menu dates can be provided. A summary of the calculated nutrient value of the menu is then compared to the nutrient standards of a selected age group and deficiencies highlighted.

• The software will search the database for food items containing specific nutrients, so that menus can be adjusted to meet the nutrient standards.

• The nutrient composition of all food items and recipes in the databases (CN Database and local database) can be printed.

• Training Documents and the User's Manual must be presented in a complete, sequential, easy-to-understand format. The developer must have a system to update the database whenever a new release of the CN Database is available.

Appendix E: Sample Nutrition Facts Label

Nutrition Facts
Serving Size 2 tortillas (51g)
Servings Per Container 6

Amount Per Serving

Calories 110   Calories from Fat 10

	% Daily Value*
Total Fat 1g	**2%**
Saturated Fat 0g	**0%**
Trans Fat 0g	
Cholesterol 0mg	**0%**
Sodium 30mg	**1%**
Total Carbohydrate 22g	**7%**
Dietary Fiber 2g	**9%**
Sugars 0g	
Protein 2g	

Vitamin A 0%	•	Vitamin C 0%
Calcium 2%	•	Iron 4%

*Percent Daily Values are based on a 2,000 calorie diet. Your daily values may be higher or lower depending on your calorie needs:

	Calories:	2,000	2,500
Total Fat	Less than	65g	80g
Saturated Fat	Less than	20g	25g
Cholesterol	Less than	300mg	300mg
Sodium	Less than	2,400mg	2,400mg
Total Carbohydrate		300g	375g
Dietary Fiber		25g	30g

Calories per gram:
    Fat 9 • Carbohydrate 4 • Protein 4

**For more information on the Nutrition Facts Label visit the FDA website at:
http://www.fda.gov/Food/IngredientsPackagingLabeling/
LabelingNutrition/ucm20026097.htm**

Appendix F: Form for Manufacturers to Submit to Have Food Products Added to CN Database

OMB APPROVED NO.
Expiration Date:

U.S. Department of Agriculture • Food and Nutrition Service

CN Database Qualification Report

According to the Paperwork Reduction Act of 1995, no persons are required to respond to a Collection of Information unless it displays a valid OMB control number. The valid OMB control number for this information collection is 0584-0494. The time required to complete this information is estimated to average 120 minutes per response, including the time to review instructions, search existing data resources, gather the data needed, and complete and review the information collection.

Date Submitted: (MM/DD/YYYY)	
Manufacturer Information: Company Name: Street1: Street2: City, State: Zip Code:	Manufacturer Information Continued: Company Website: Company Phone: (xxx) yyy-**zzzz**: Company Fax: (xxx) yyy-**zzzz**: General Email:

MFR Product Name: (Max 255 characters-example: Pizza, pepperoni topping, regular crust, frozen, cooked)

Product Name Shortened:(Max 60 characters-example: pepperoni pizza)	Brand: (Max 40 characters)
Unit UPC: (12 numbers) __ - __ __ __ __ __ - __ __ __ __ __ - __	Product Number/Code:
Food Category Code: (from table on field explanation page 3)	Product Is Produced For School Food Service? ☐ YES ☐ NO

Product Is Produced With USDA Commodity Food?   ☐ YES ☐ NO

NLEA Adjusted Values: ☐ YES ☐ NO

Value Type Code: Analytical Data (A), USDA Data (U), Calculated Data (C)   ☐ A ☐ U ☐ C

As Served (S) or As Purchased (P):   ☐ S   ☐ P
Is This An Enriched Or Fortified Product?   ☐ YES ☐ NO

Notes:

_____
_____
_____
_____

FNS-710 (12-13) Previous Editions Obsolete   SBU   Electronic Form Version Designed in Adobe 9.1 Version

Pre-Publication Copy

Product Number/Code (from page one):	Household Serving Amount: (a numeric value)
Household Serving Measure Description: (Example: Cup, Ounce, Patty, Piece, Slice)	Household Serving Size In Grams or Ounce: _____ g or _____ oz

Nutrient Serving Size (Total Gram Weight Of Product Upon Which The Following Nutrients Are Based):_____g
(Ounce To Gram Conversion Factor: Ounce X 28.35g/oz = Grams)

Total Calories: _____Kcal (Calories)   *Vitamin A: _____IU or _____% DV

*Total Fat: _____g   *Sugars: _____g

Saturated Fat: _____g   *Vitamin C: _____mg or _____% DV

*Trans Fat: _____g   *Iron: _____mg or _____% DV

*Cholesterol: _____mg   *Calcium: _____mg or _____% DV

Sodium: _____mg   *Water (Moisture): _____g

*Total Carbohydrate: _____g   *Ash: _____g

*Total Dietary Fiber: _____g

*Protein: _____g   * It Is Optional To List Values For These Nutrients

LIST OF INGREDIENTS:

_____
_____
_____
_____
_____
_____
_____
_____
_____
_____
_____
_____
_____
_____
_____
_____
_____
_____
_____
_____
_____
_____

CN Qualification Report Field Explanation

Enter the **Date Submitted**, and **Manufacturer Information**. The **MFR Product Name** should follow the naming convention used in the USDA's National Nutrient Database for Standard Reference (﹛HYPERLINK "http://www.nal.usda.gov/fnic/foodcomp/search/"﹜). The **Product Name Shortened** should not be an abbreviation of each word in the full product name but rather should be a clear and concise shortened version of the full product name. The **Brand** for the product should be listed separately from the full or shortened product name. The **Unit UPC** is the 12 digit Universal Product Code and is important for correctly matching the information to the product. Example: 0 - 12345 - 12345 - 0. The **Product Number/Code** should be your product's 5 digit UPC# (The portion after the second dash) if you do not use a separate product number or code. The **Food Category Code** comes from a USDA Table. Please select from the following list of 2-digit categories.

Food Category Codes

01	Dairy: butter, cheese, eggs, milk, yogurt	16	Condiments: catsup, mustard, relish
02	Spice: seasonings, flavorings, leavening agents	17	Lamb, veal and game products
03	Baby food	18	Baked goods: bread, cakes, cookies, crackers, pies, rolls
04	Fats & Oils: margarine, shortening, mayonnaise, salad dressings	19	Sweets
		20	Grains
05	Poultry Products	21	Fast Foods
06	Soups, Sauces and Gravies	22	Meals, Entrees, and Sidedishes
07	Luncheon meat & sausage	25	Snacks
08	Breakfast Cereals	29	Miscellaneous
09	Fruits and fruit juices		
10	Pork Products	30 - 39	Reserved for USDA Recipes
11	Vegetables: includes beans & legumes		
12	Nuts and seeds	43	Purchased mixed dishes: lunch entries
13	Beef	44	Purchased mixed dishes: breakfast entrees
14	Beverages	45	Meat substitute/Vegetable proteins
15	Fish		

Indicate whether the product is or is not intended for **School Food Service** and whether it is or is not produced with **USDA Commodity Food**. Indicate whether the nutritional information is based on the **Nutrition Labeling and Education Act (NLEA) Adjusted Values** (Nutrition Facts data).

Select your **Value Type Code** from the following list based on the nutrient data you are reporting: A= Analytical -laboratory data; U = USDA - from a USDA database; C = Calculated - from nutrition facts panel or from individual ingredients.

Indicate whether the nutritional information provided is on an **As Served** or **As Purchased** basis and whether or not the product is **Enriched/Fortified**. There is a space for **Notes** if needed.

Repeat the **Product Number/Code** from page one so that page two can be matched up if necessary. The **Household Serving Amount** is a numeric value used to describe the amount of a specific **Household Serving Measure Description**. The two combined make up the **Household Serving Size**. The **Household Serving Measure Description** should be chosen from the following list of abbreviations:

CM	Centimeter	MG	Milligram (1000th of gram)
CUP	Cup (volume: sometimes fluid; 1 cup = 8 fluid ounces)	ML	Milliliter (volume; usually fluid)
FT	Feet (dimension)	OZ	Ounce (weight; 16 ounces = 1 pound)
GAL	Gallon (volume: sometimes fluid)	FL OZ	Fluid Ounce (volume; 8 fluid ounces = 1 cup)
GM	Gram (weight)	PACKAGE	Package/Box/Case/Bag
IN	Inch (dimension; 12 inch = 1 foot)	PIECE	Piece/Portion/Unit/Item/Serving
KG	Kilogram (weight; 1 kg = 1000 grams)	PT	Pint (volume: sometimes fluid)
LB	Pound (weight)	QT	Quart (volume: sometimes fluid; 4 quarts = 1 gallon)
LT	Liter (volume; usually fluid)	TBSP	Tablespoon (volume; 16 tablespoons = 1 cup)
M	Meter (dimension)	TSP	Teaspoon (volume; 3 teaspoon = 1 tablespoon)

The **Nutrient Serving Size** in grams may be equivalent to the **Household Serving Size** or the net weight on a single serve package if you are reporting Nutrition Facts (NLEA) data. For example, if the **Nutrient Serving Size** is based on one 57 gram single serve package, then the **Household Serving Amount** plus the **Household Serving Measure Description** (=Household Serving Size) would be 2.0 OZ for a non-liquid product. 57 grams divided by 28.35 grams per ounce equals the **Household Serving Size** of 2.0 ounces. Provide the nutrient values in the appropriate units designated in the nutrient list. Nutrients listed with an asterisk are **Optional**; Lastly, provide a **List of Ingredients** found in the product by order of predominance.

APPENDIX G
Raw-To-Cooked Conversion Factor for Selected Vegetables

Food Item (Raw, Ready-To-Cook)	Yield (cooked)
Apples, cored, cut or whole	.85
Asparagus, trimmed	.94
Beets, pared	.94
Cabbage, Green, cored	.94
Carrots, sliced	.91
Cauliflower, stemmed	.98
Celery, trimmed	.89
Chayote (Mirliton), pitted, sliced	.91
Jicama (Yam Bean), peeled, julienned	.97
Malanga (Taro), peeled, diced	1.20
Onions, peeled, cut	.88
Pepper, Bell, stemmed, seeded, cut	.91
Potato, pared	.91
Squash, Yellow, trimmed, sliced	.87
Tomatillo, stemmed, diced	.83
Turnips, pared, cubed	.93
Yautia (Tannier), peeled, diced	1.00
Zucchini, trimmed, cubed	.90

APPENDIX H
Common Moisture and Fat Change Values (%) for Purchased Prepared Foods that are Fried

Food Item	Moisture Change %	Fat Change %
Burrito	-11%	+9.5%
Chicken, Nuggets, or Patties, breaded or battered, pre-fried, frozen	-10%	+4%
Corn Dogs, pre-fried, frozen	-8%	+2.5%
Fish Nuggets, portions, Sticks, breaded or battered, oil-blanched, frozen	-10%	+4%
Funnel Cake, from mix	-31%	+10%
Hush Puppies, pre-fried, oil-blanched, frozen	-8%	+2.5%
Potatoes, French-fried, oil-blanched, frozen	-27.5%	+3.5%
Potatoes, Chopped, and Formed, Rounds and Nuggets, oil-blanched, frozen	-5%	+3.5%
Steak, Chicken Fried, pre-fried, frozen	-10%	+2.5%
Taco Shell, Flour, for Taco Salad	-22%	+19%
Vegetables, battered or breaded (eggplant, okra, squash, etc.)	-20%	+8%

www.ingramcontent.com/pod-product-compliance
Lightning Source LLC
Chambersburg PA
CBHW080835180526
45168CB00006B/2693